# THE OXFORDSHIRE
## COLOURING BOOK

First published 2017

The History Press
The Mill, Brimscombe Port
Stroud, Gloucestershire, GL5 2QG
www.thehistorypress.co.uk

Text © The History Press, 2017
Illustrations by Sally Townsend © The History Press, 2017

The right of The History Press to be identified as the Author
of this work has been asserted in accordance with the
Copyright, Designs and Patents Act 1988.

All rights reserved. No part of this book may be reprinted
or reproduced or utilised in any form or by any electronic,
mechanical or other means, now known or hereafter invented,
including photocopying and recording, or in any information storage or
retrieval system, without the permission in writing from the Publishers.

British Library Cataloguing in Publication Data.
A catalogue record for this book is available from the British Library.

ISBN 978 0 7509 8001 2

Typesetting and origination by The History Press
Printed and bound in Great Britain by TJ International Ltd

# THE OXFORDSHIRE
## COLOURING BOOK

PAST AND PRESENT

Take some time out of your busy life to relax and unwind with this feel-good colouring book designed for everyone who loves Oxfordshire.

Absorb yourself in the simple action of colouring in the scenes and settings from around the county, past and present. From iconic architecture to picturesque vistas, you are sure to find some of your favourite locations waiting to be transformed with a splash of colour.

There are no rules – choose any page and any choice of colouring pens or pencils you like to create your own unique, colourful and creative illustrations.

Christ Church College and Cathedral, Oxford ▶

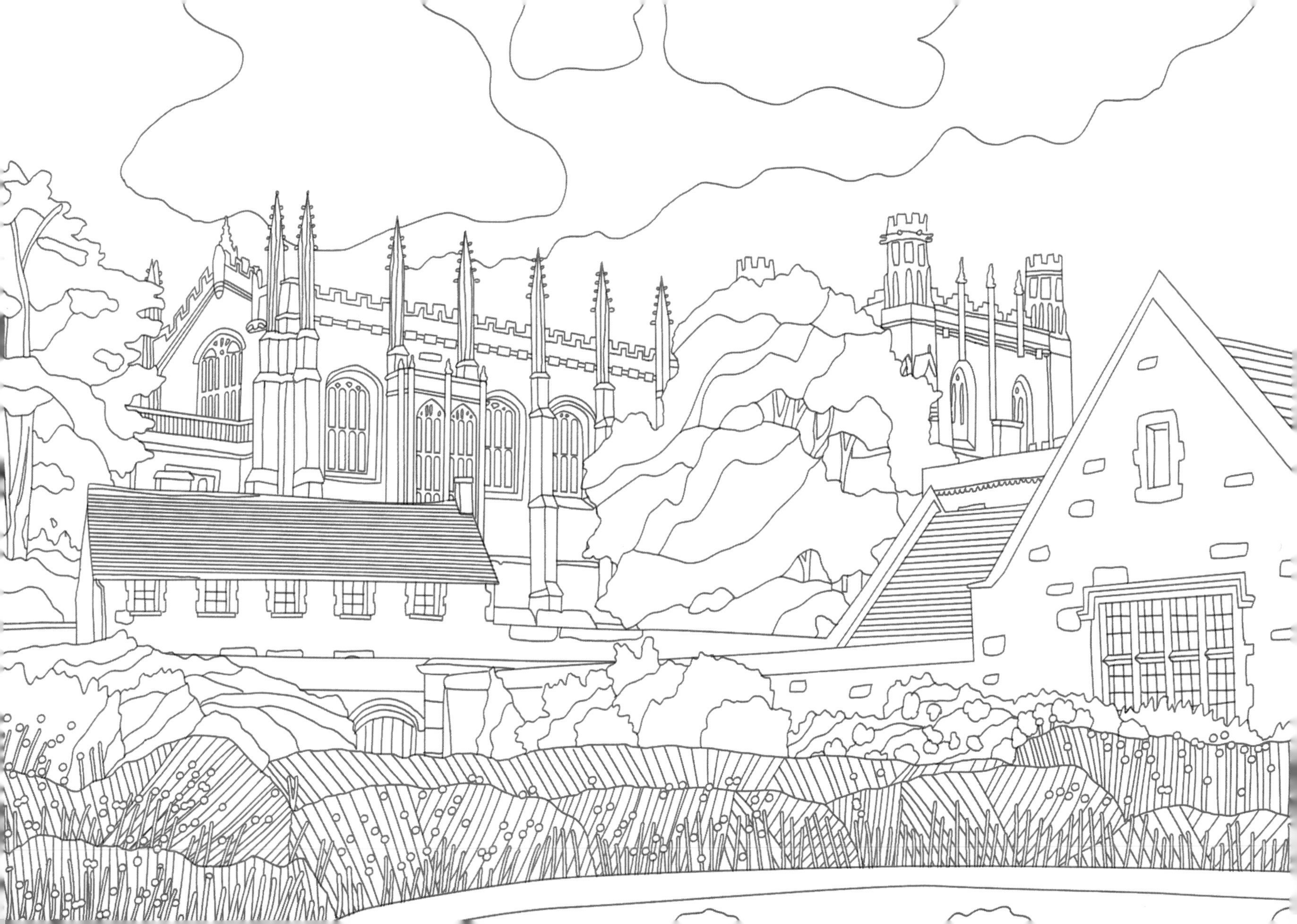

Ashmolean Museum, Oxford ▶

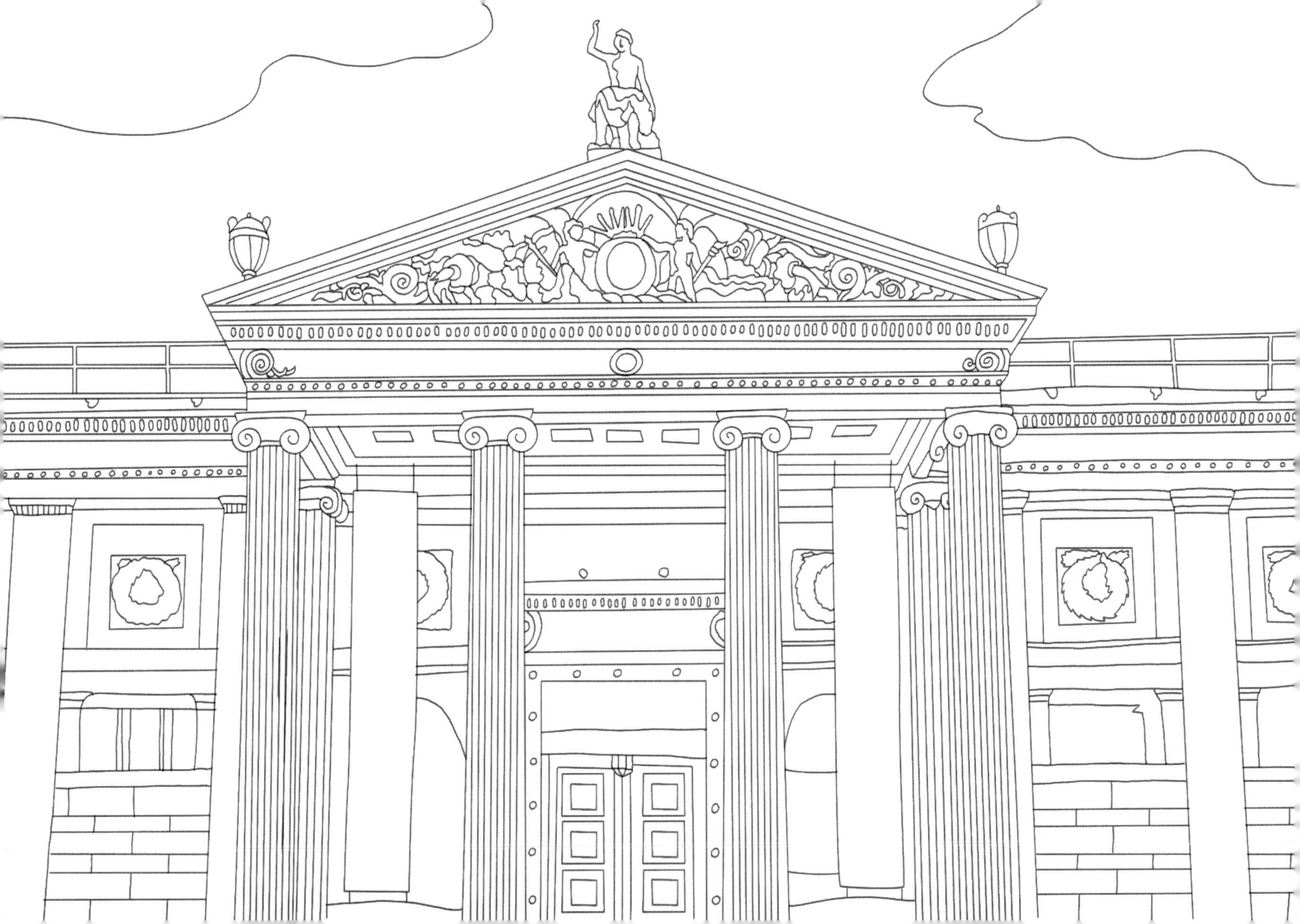

Banbury Cross, 1930s ▶

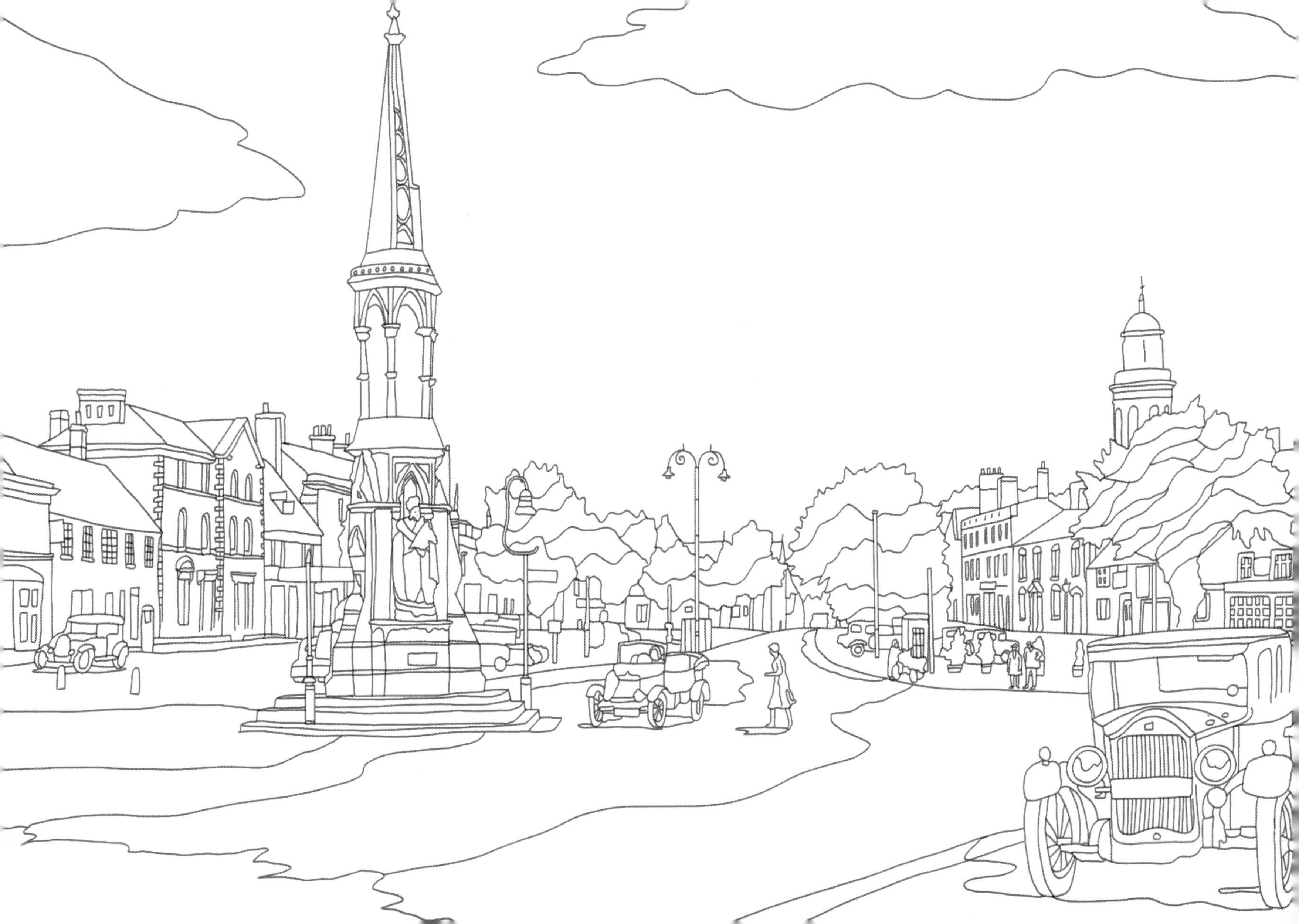

Blenheim Palace, Woodstock ▶

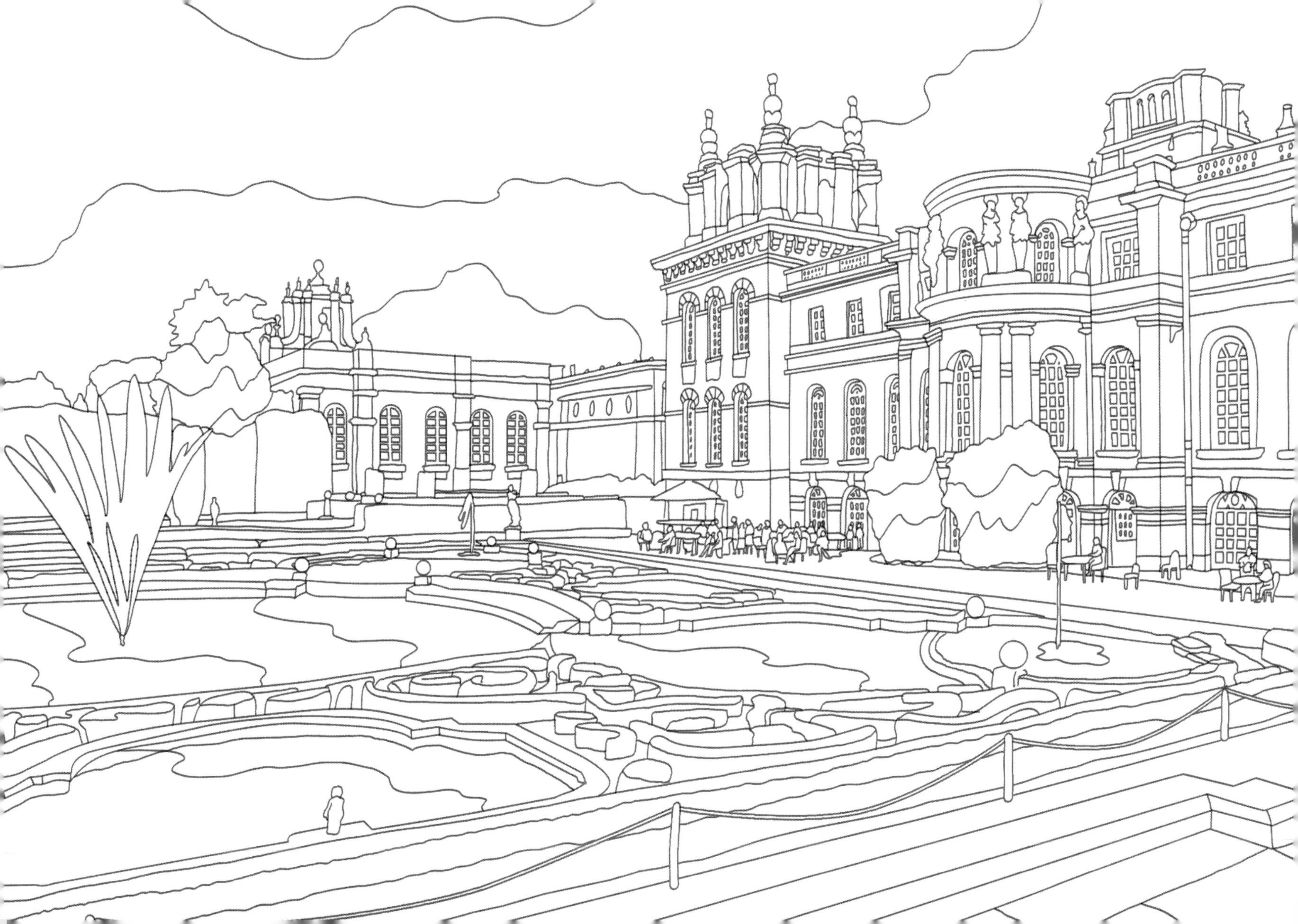

BMC 1800s on the assembly line at Cowley ▸

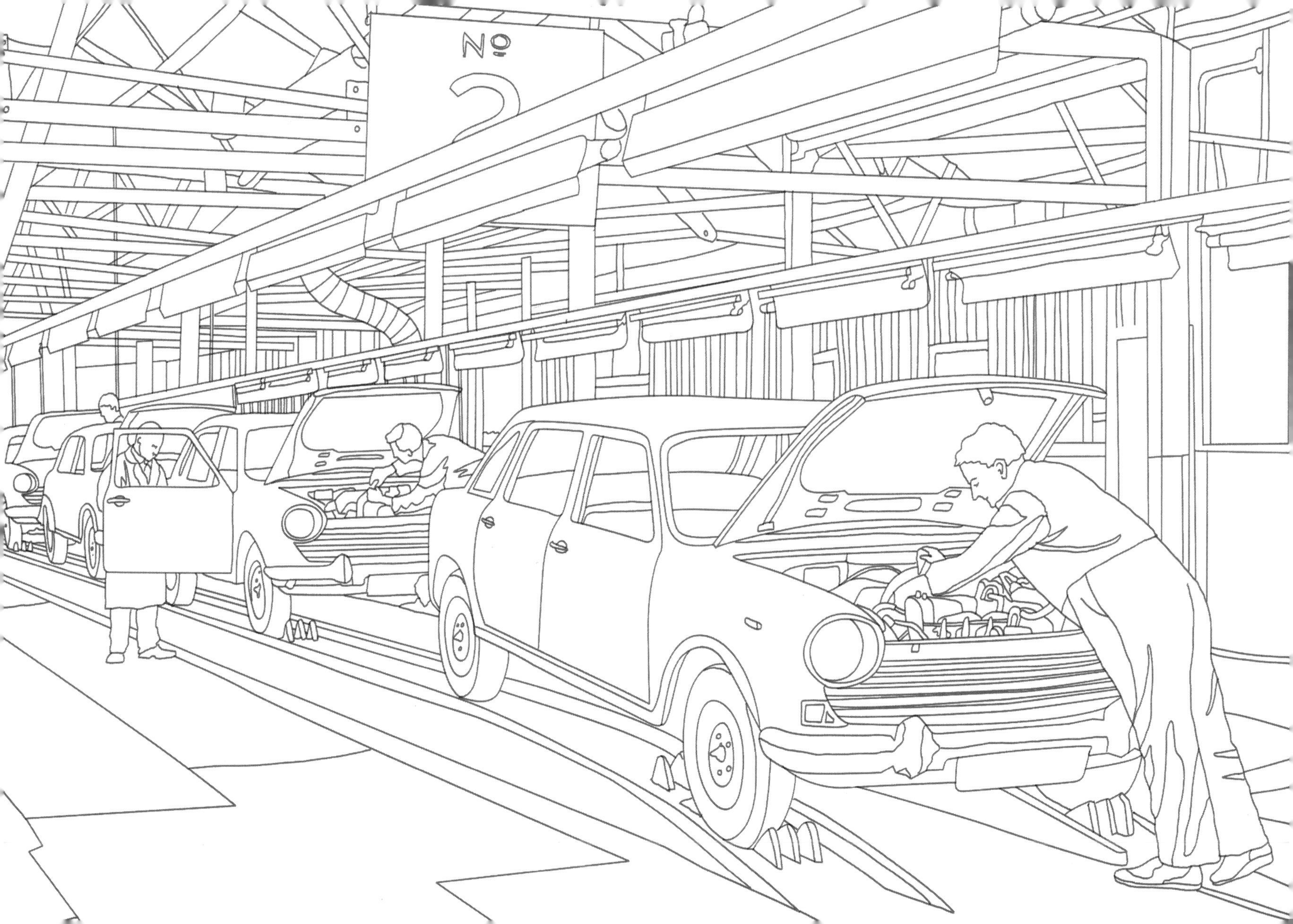
Nº
2

Brasenose College, University of Oxford ▸

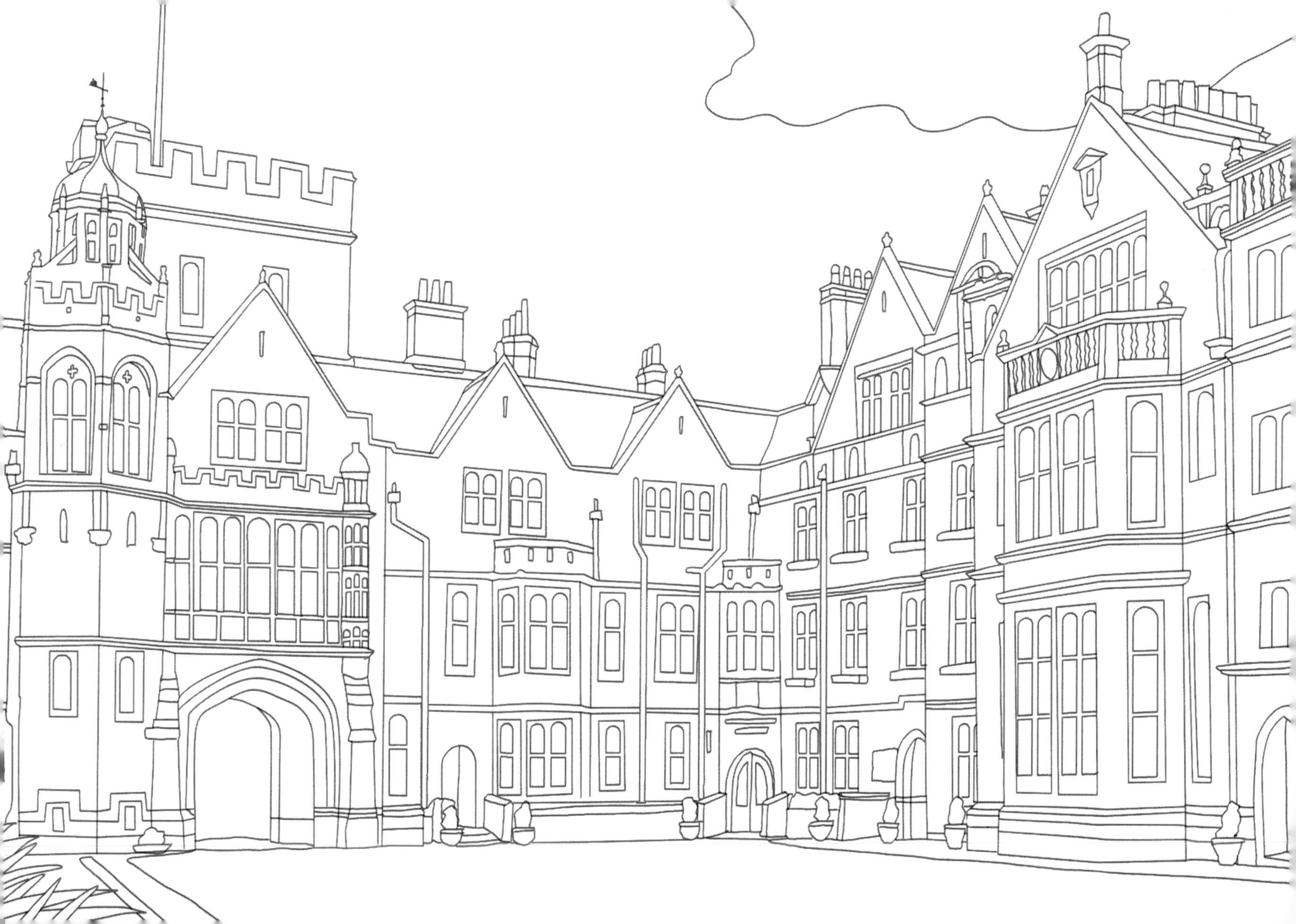

Burford ▶

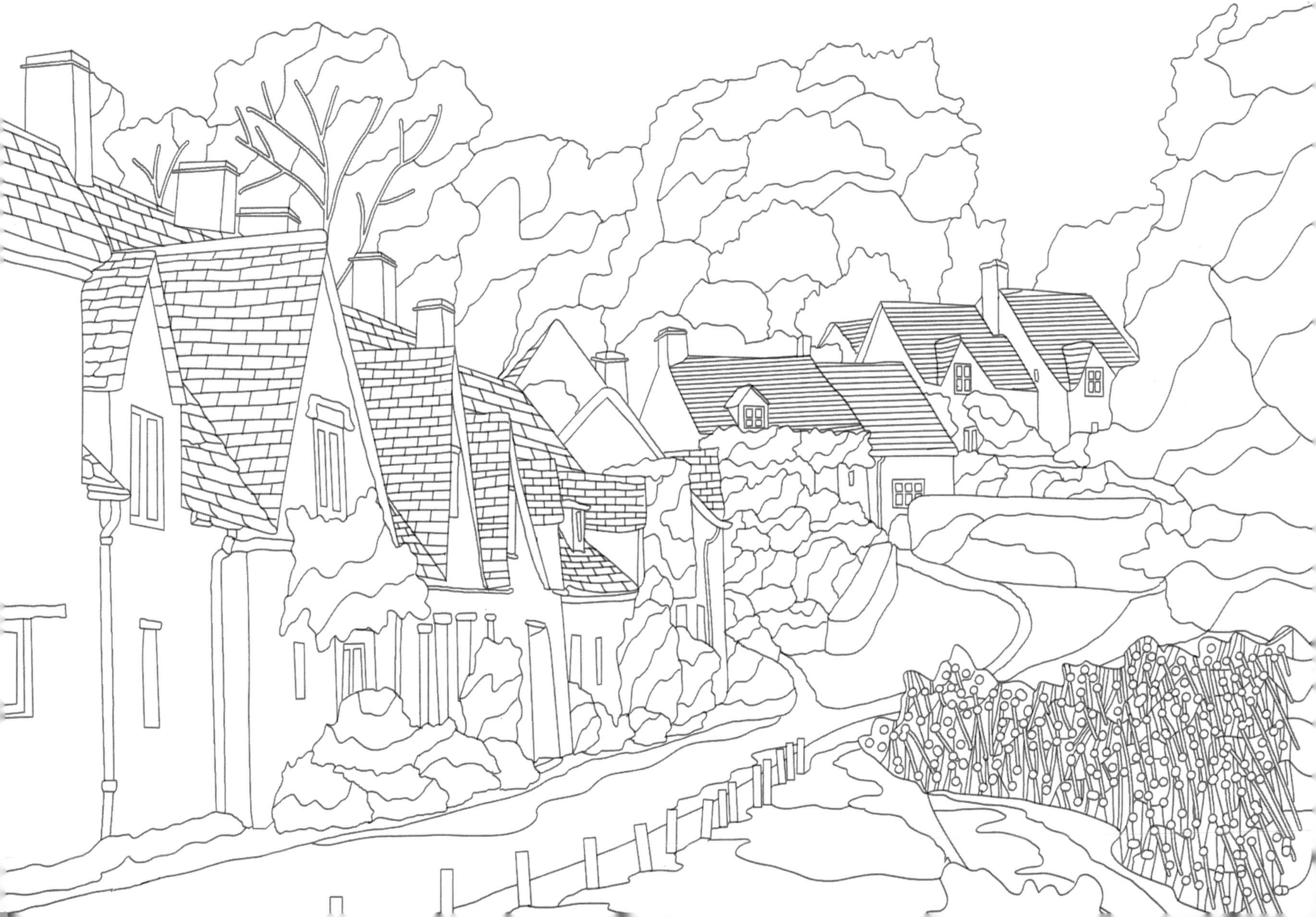

All Souls College, University of Oxford ▸

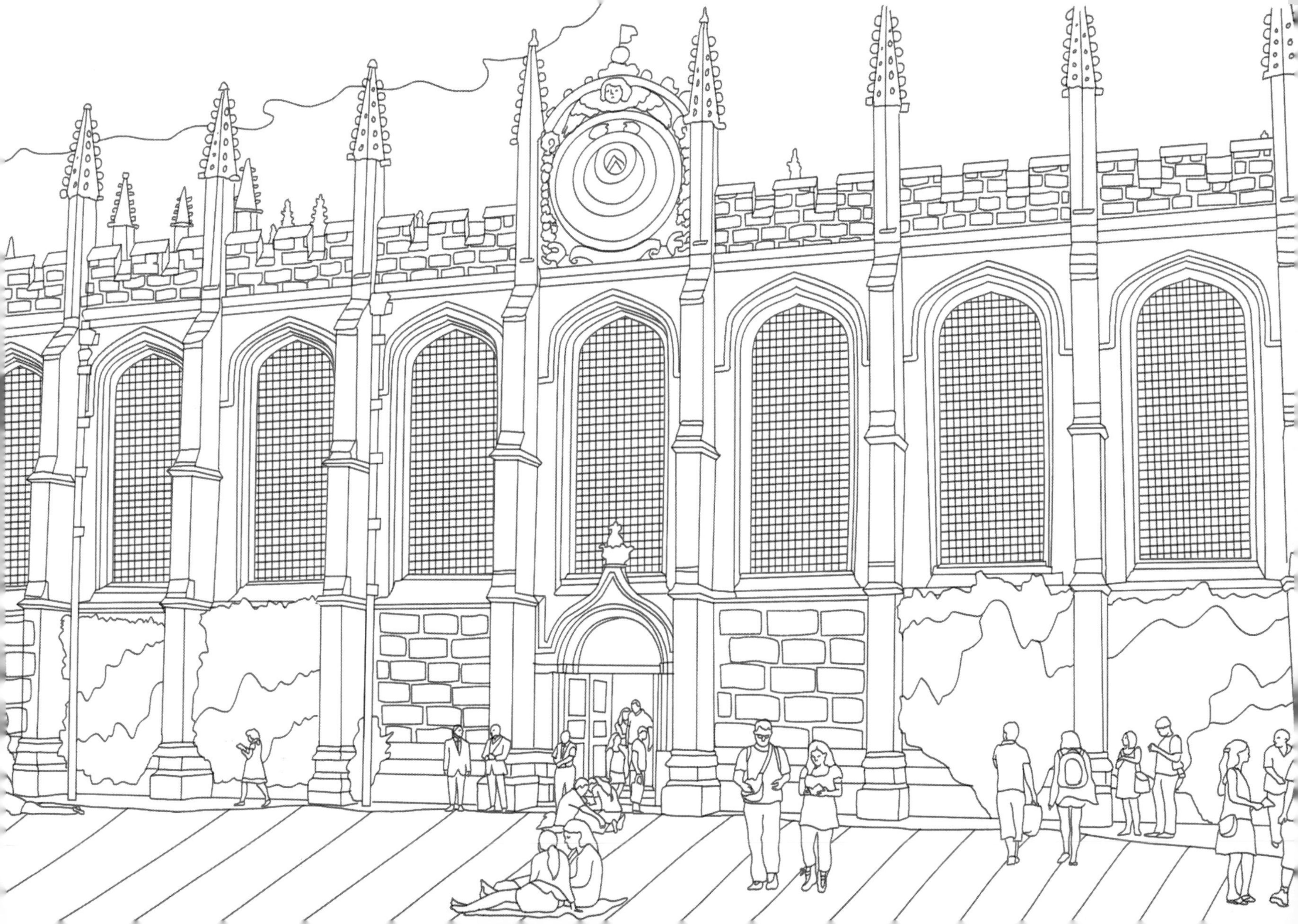

A brewer's toast outside Hook Norton Brewery in 1971 ▸

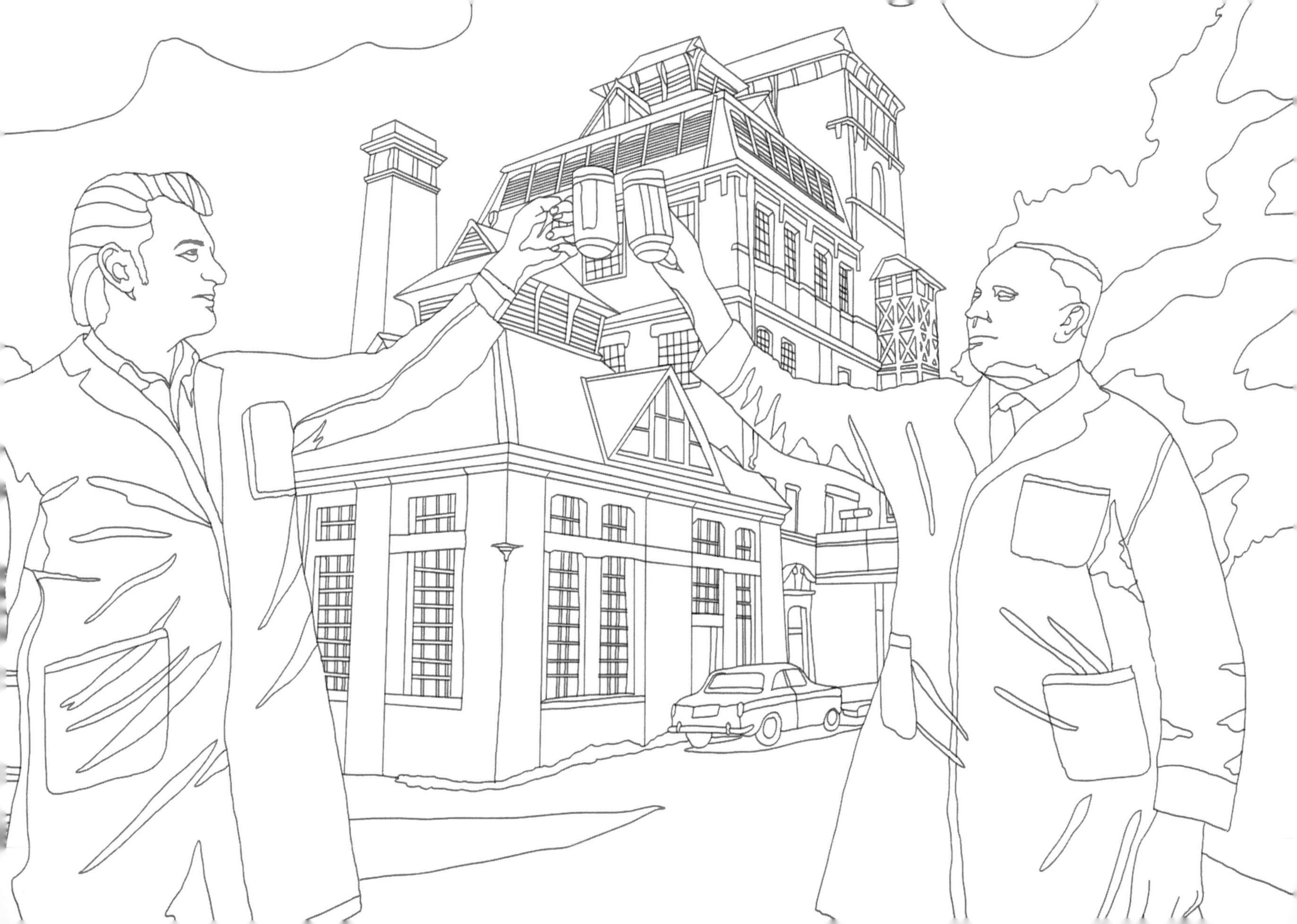

Cogges Manor Farm, Witney ▶

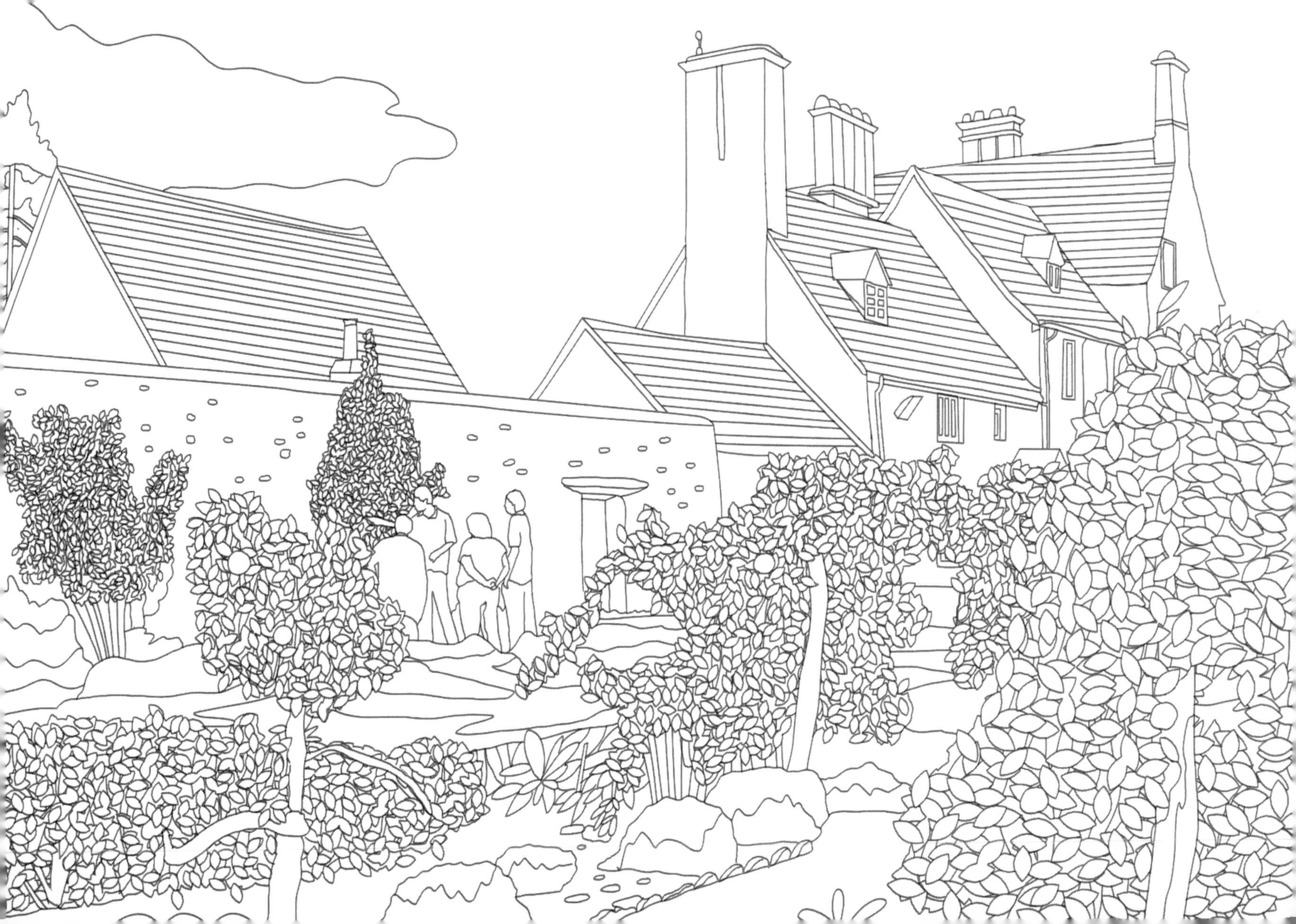

A barge on the Oxford Canal ▶

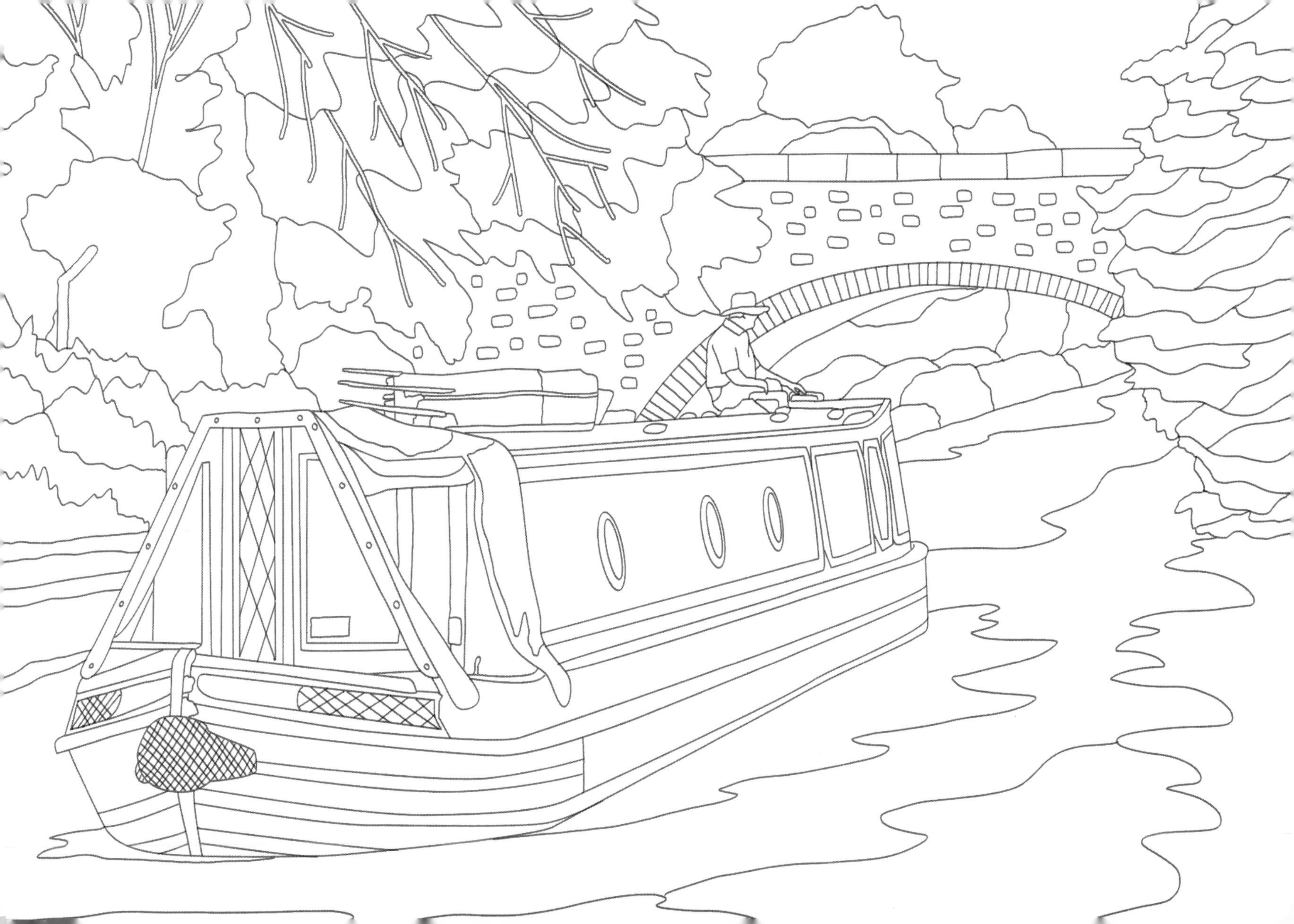

Cornmarket Street, Oxford ▶

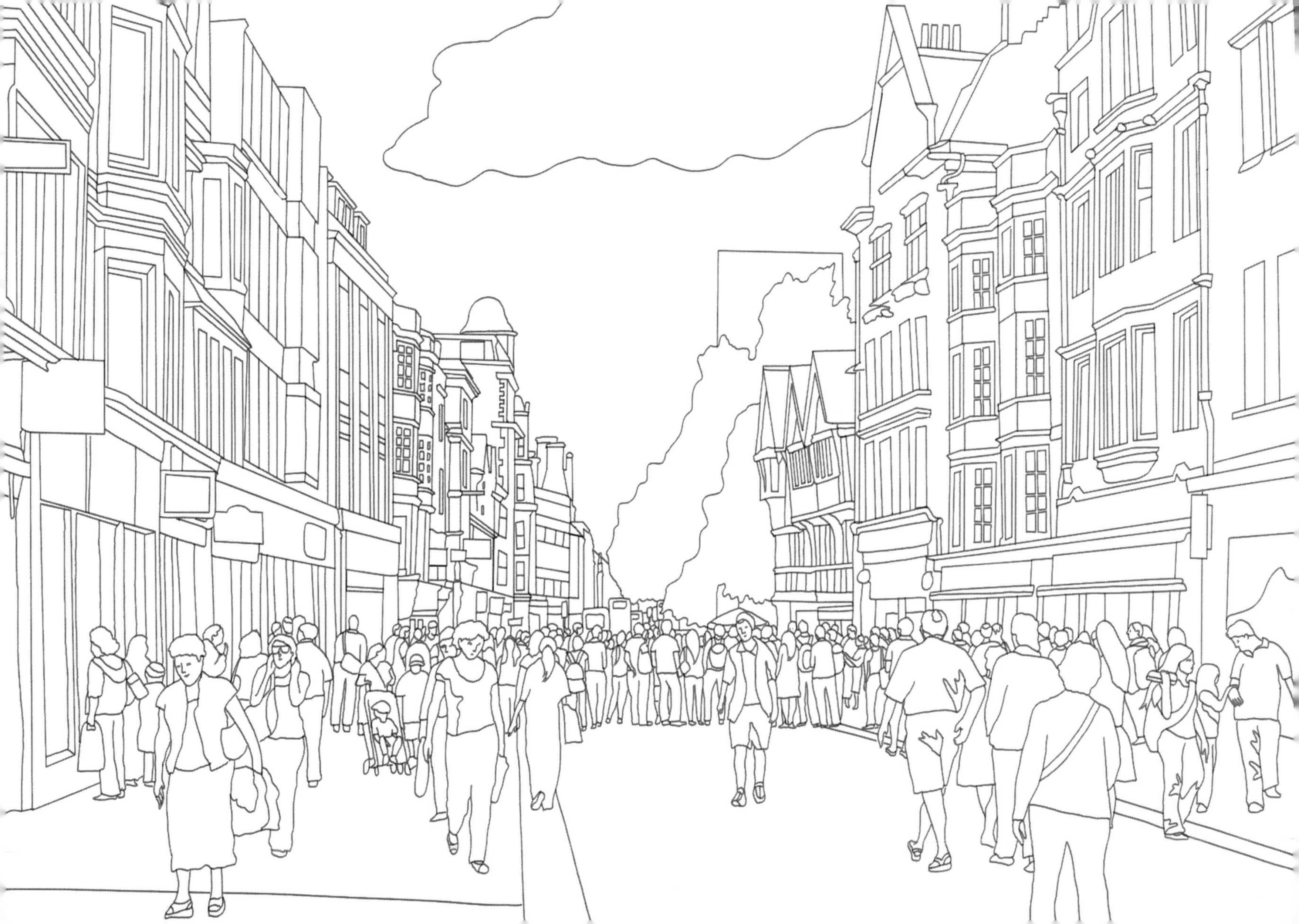

Bicycles are a popular form of transport in Oxford ▶

MAGDALEN STREET

Great Haseley Windmill ▶

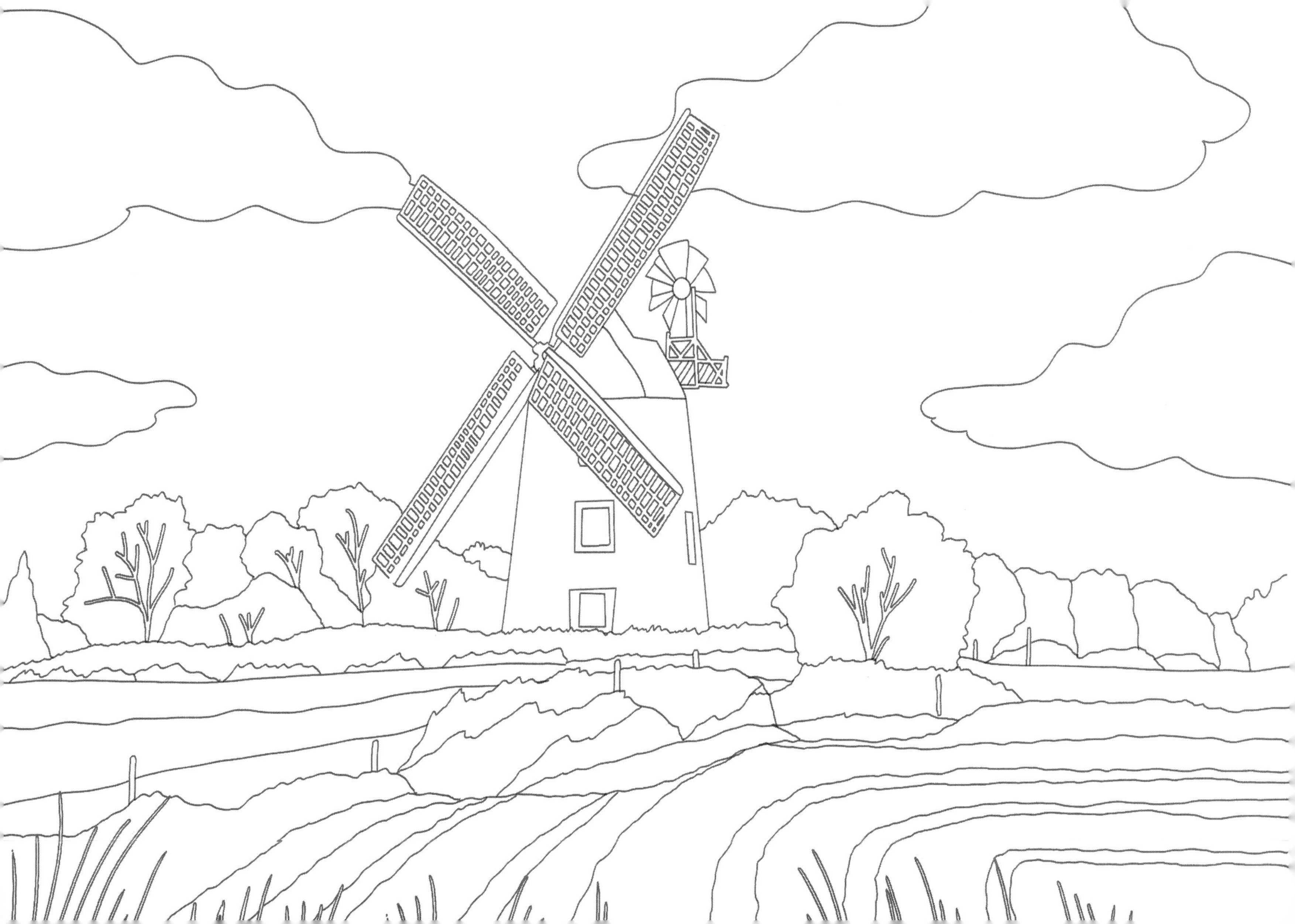

Greys Court, near Henley-on-Thames ▶

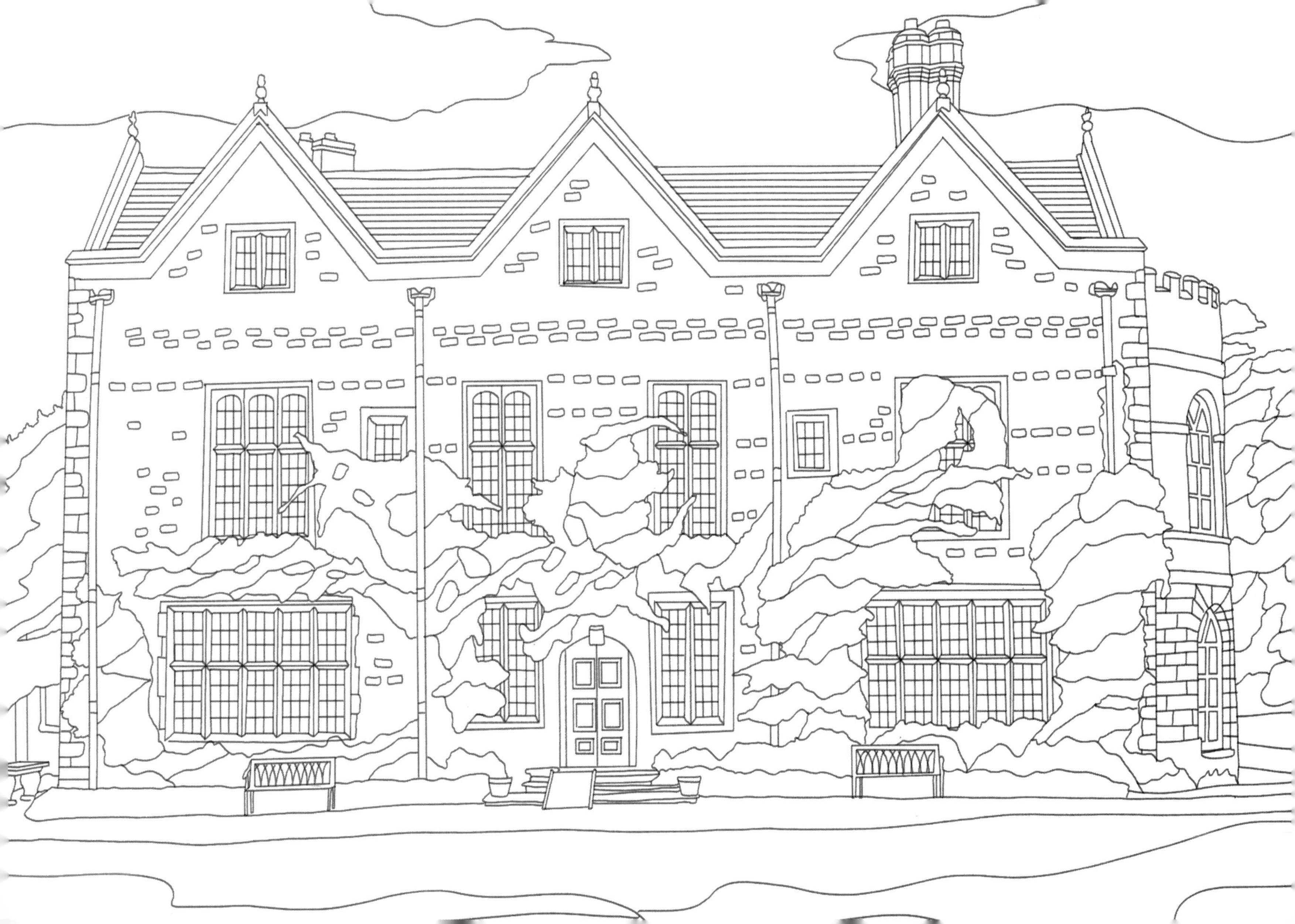

H. Boswell & Co. Ltd on Broad Street, Oxford, 1962 ▸

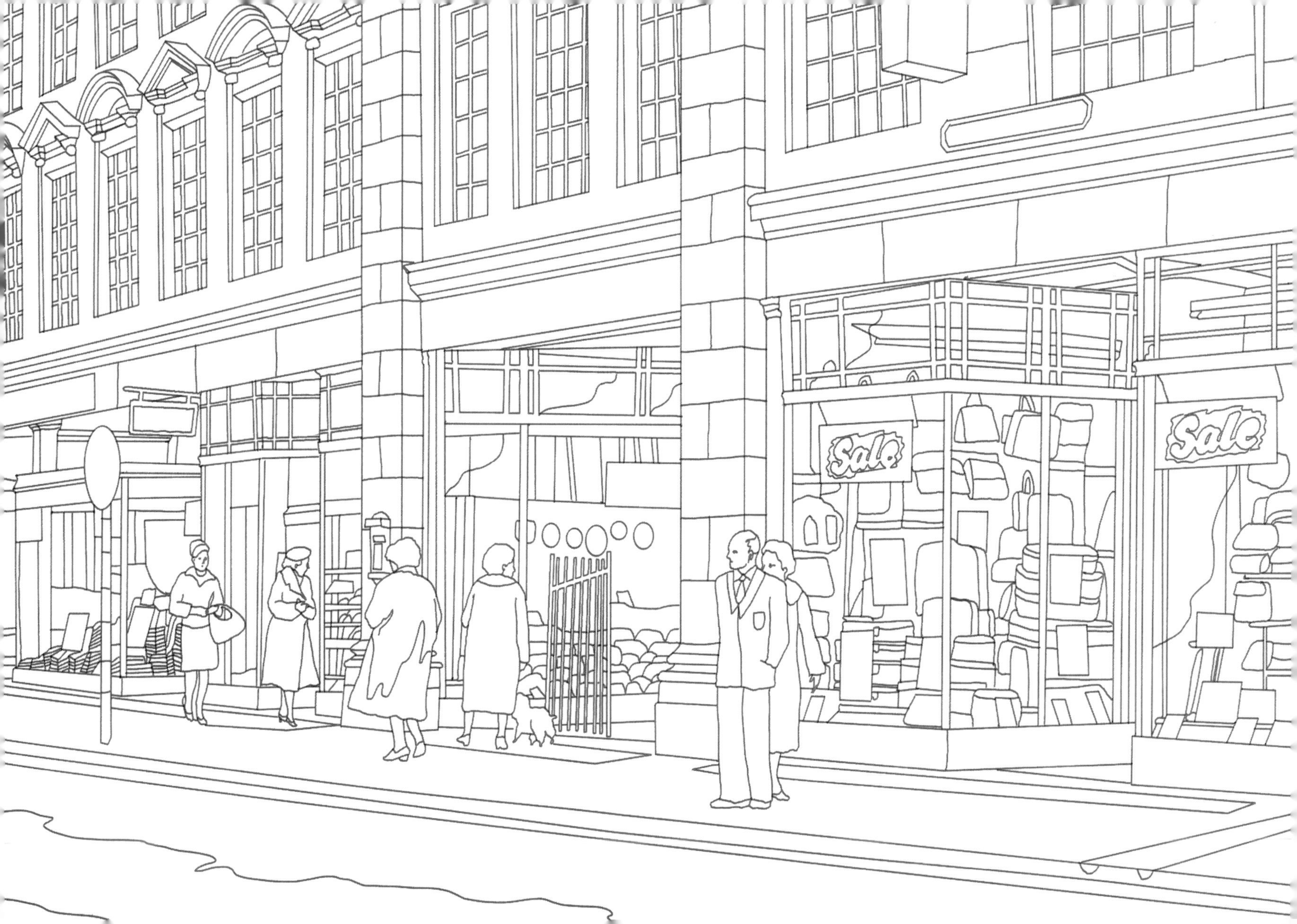
Sale
Sale

Henley-on-Thames ▶

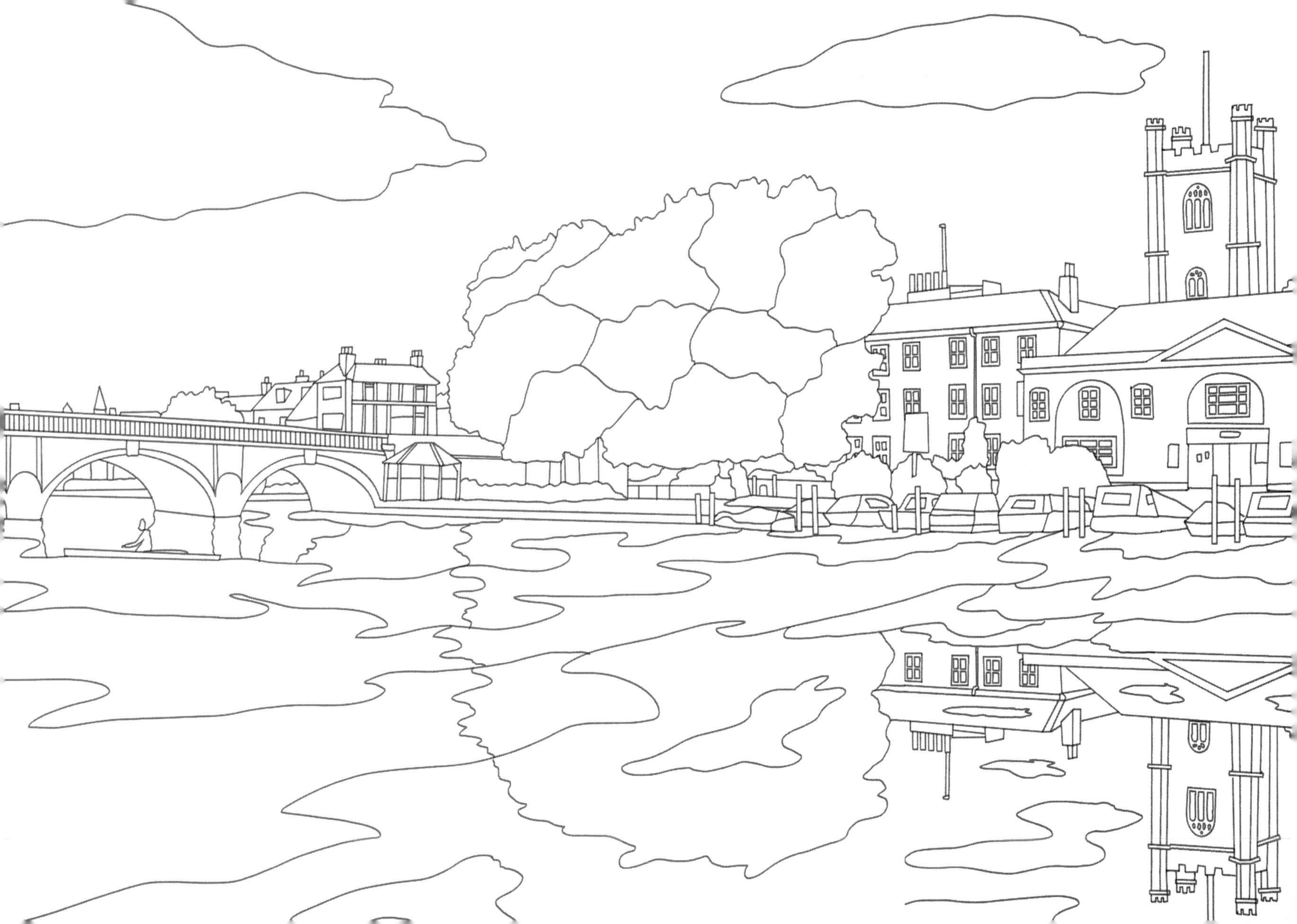

Lemurs at Cotswold Wildlife Park, Burford ▸

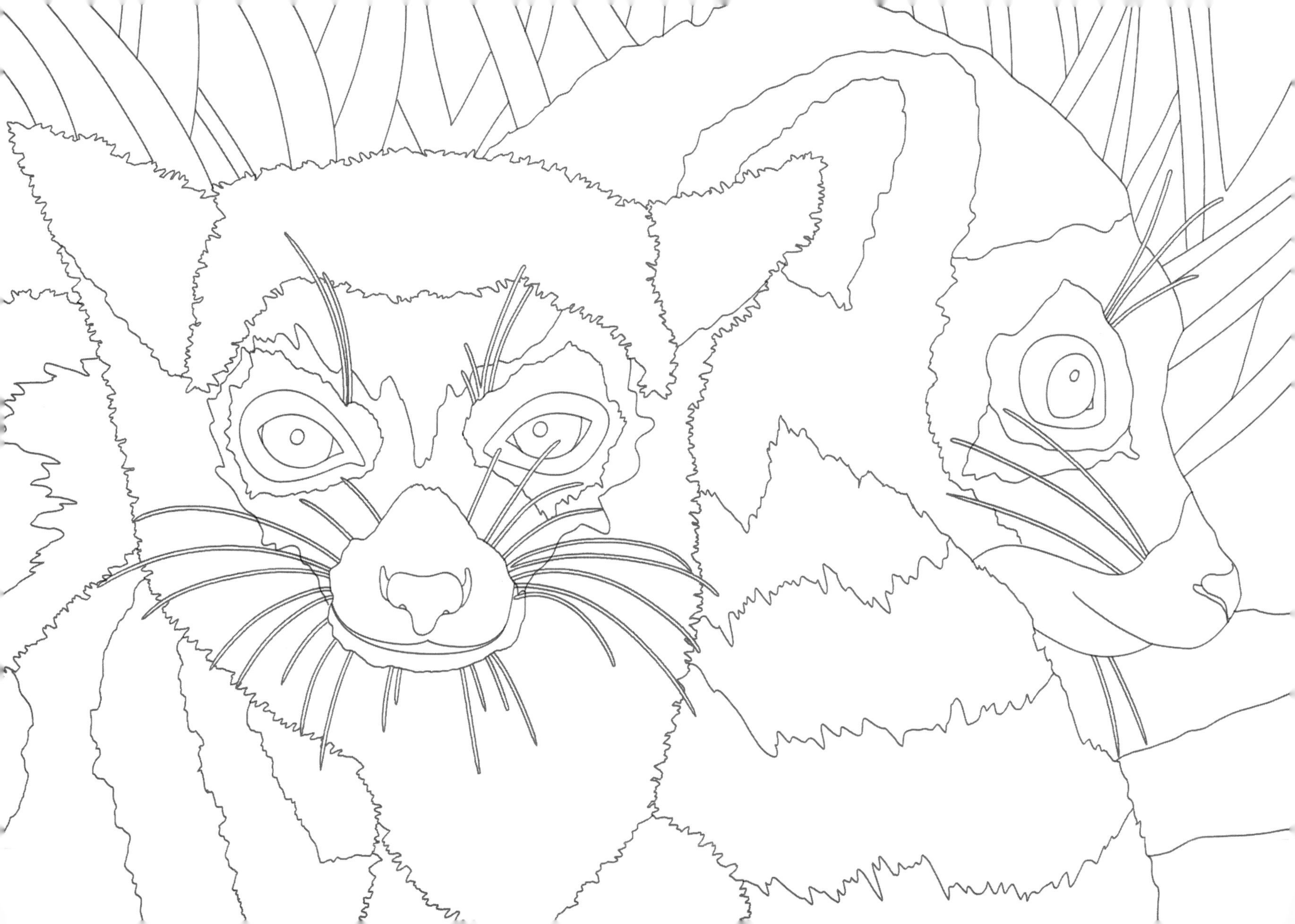

Mill Street, Witney, 1950s ▶

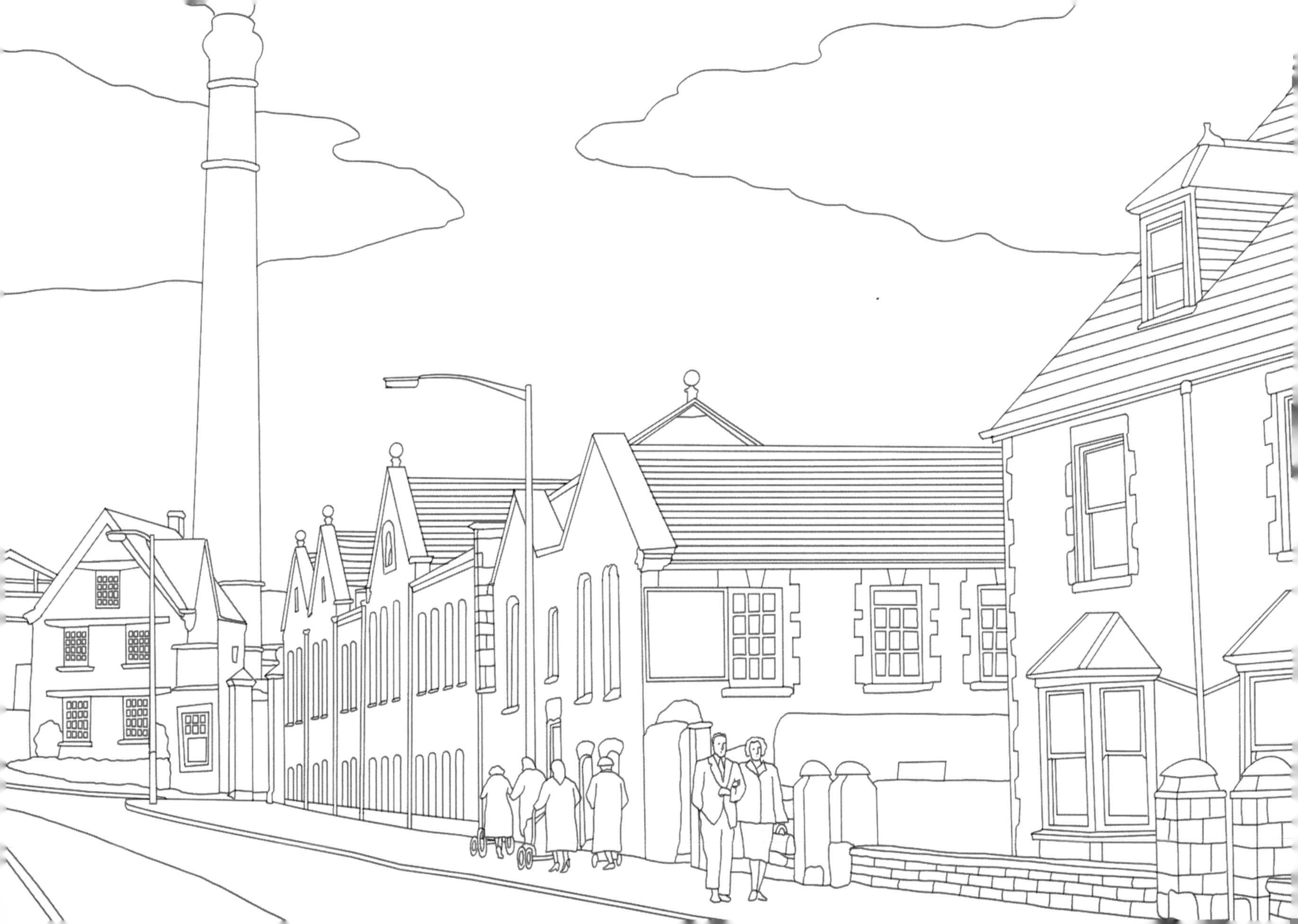

Oxford Botanic Garden ▶

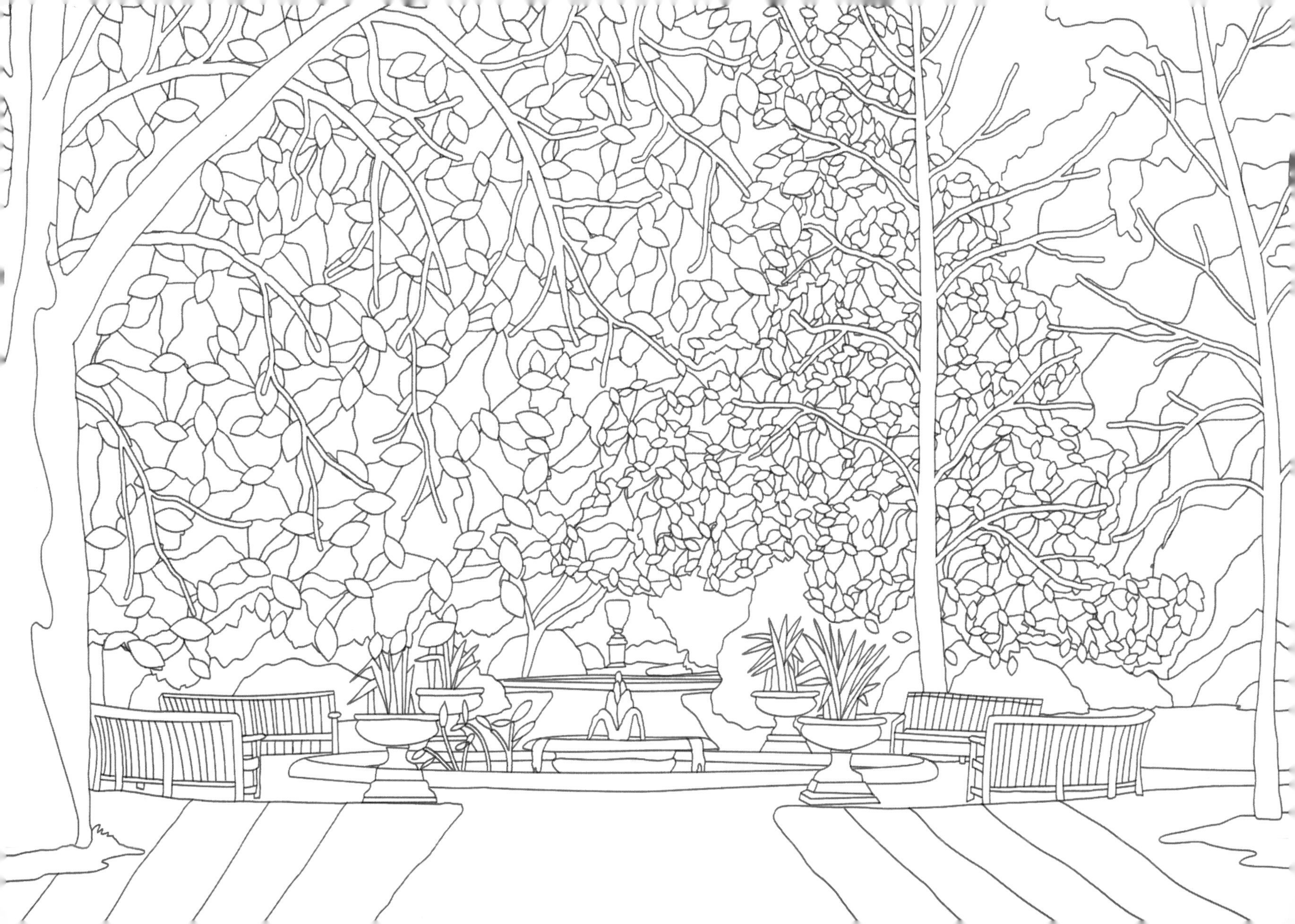

Oxford Castle ▶

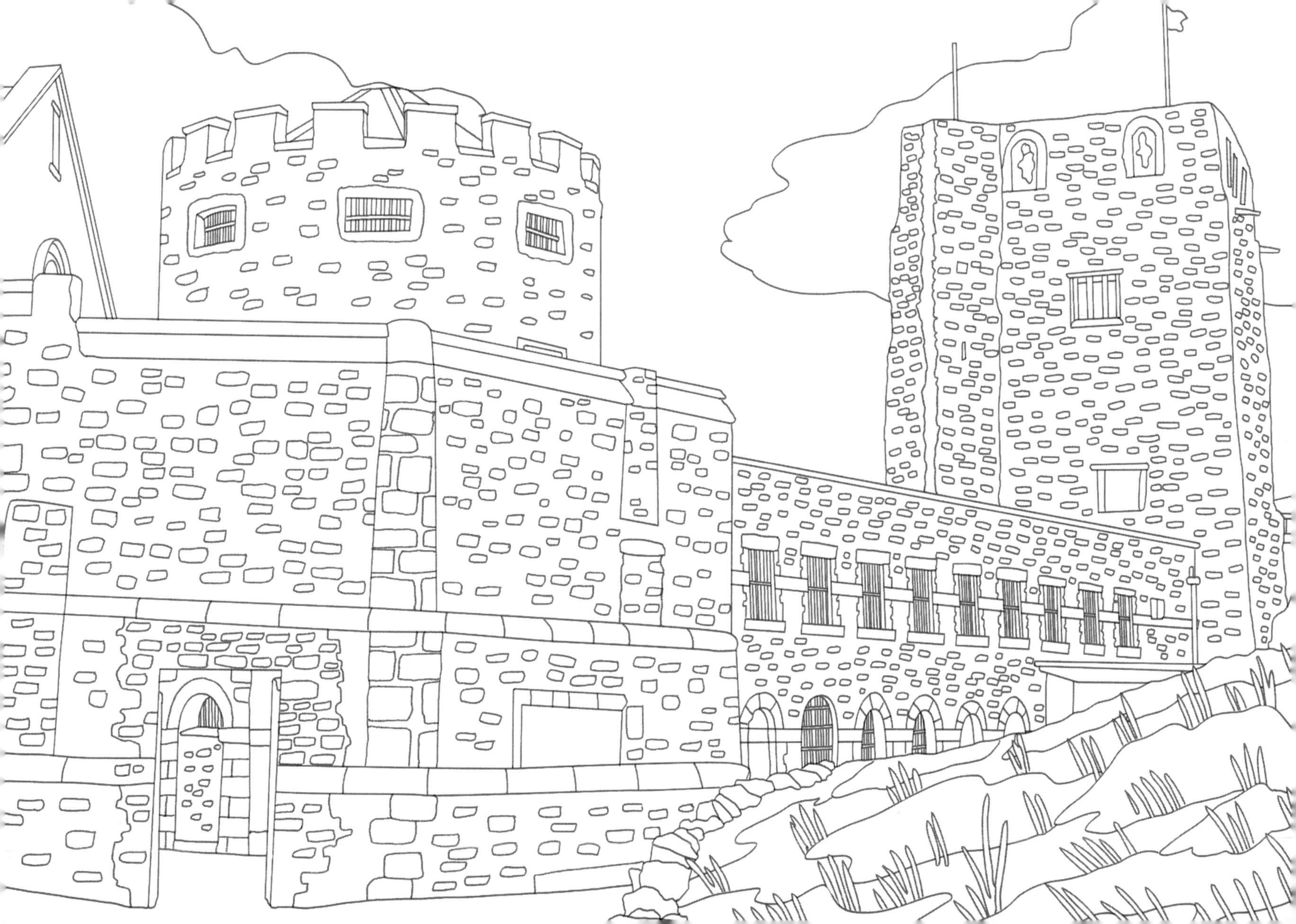

University of Oxford undergraduates
celebrate finishing their exams in 1965 ▸

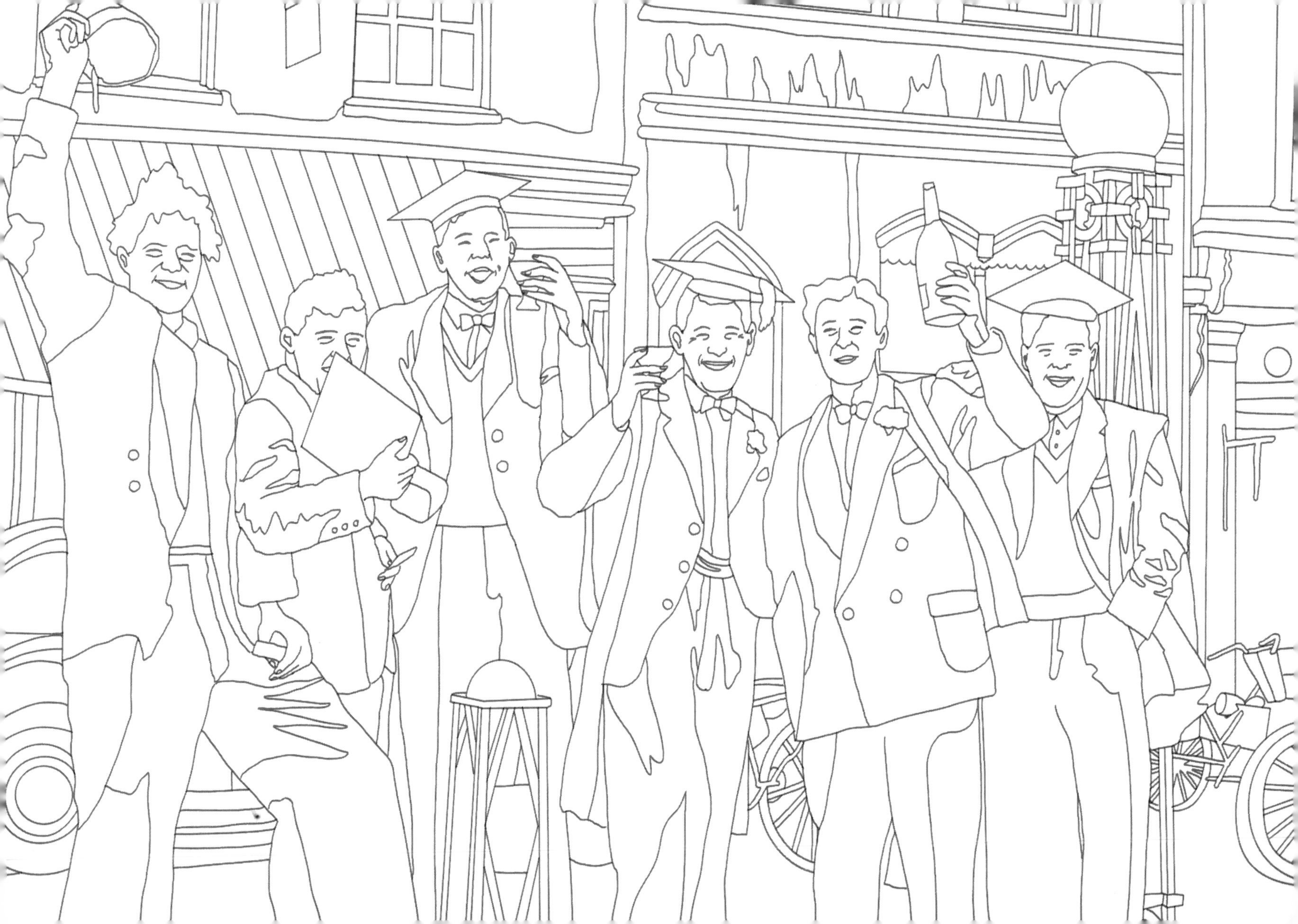

The Sheldonian Theatre, Oxford ▶

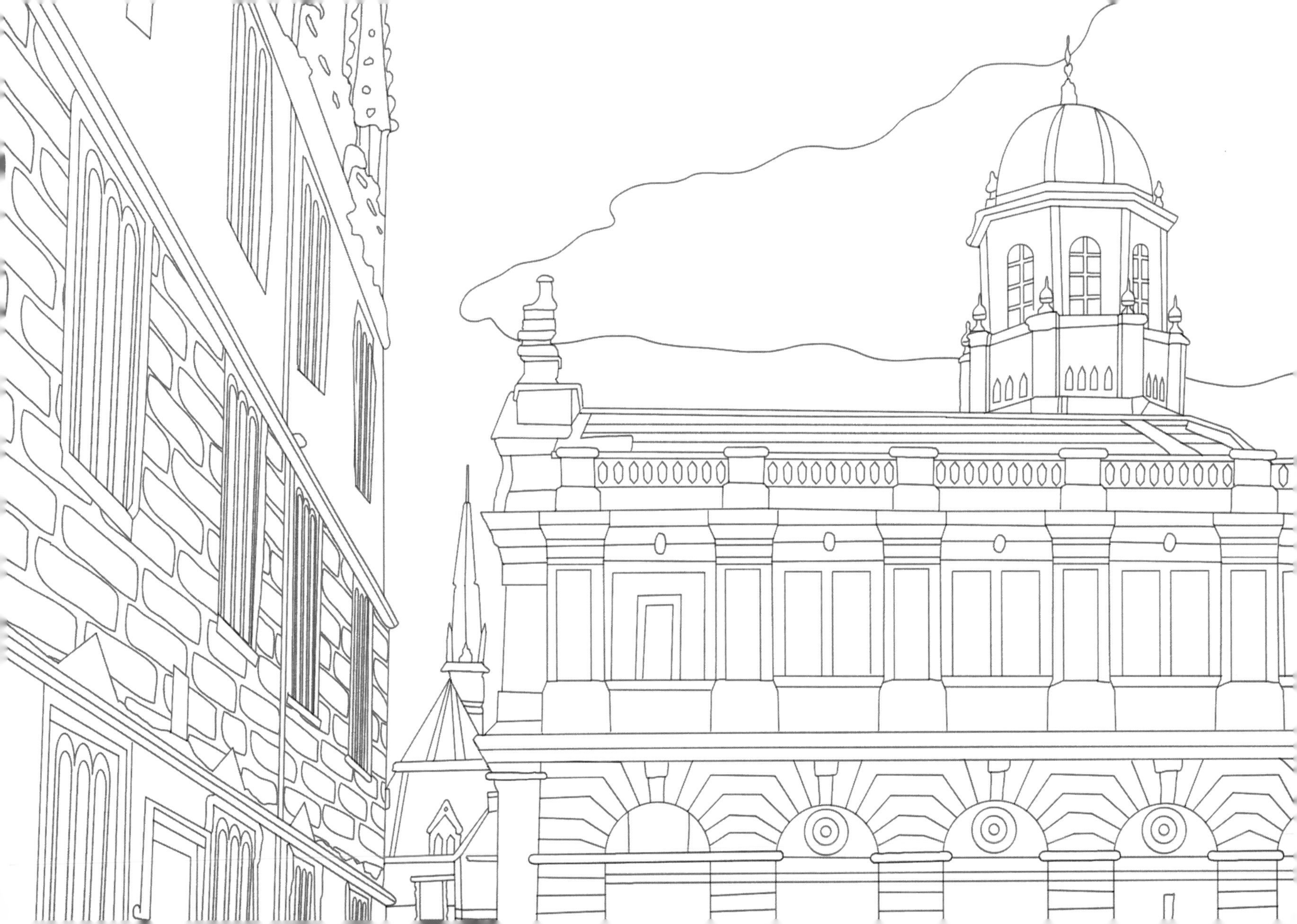

Chipping Norton and Bliss Mill ▶

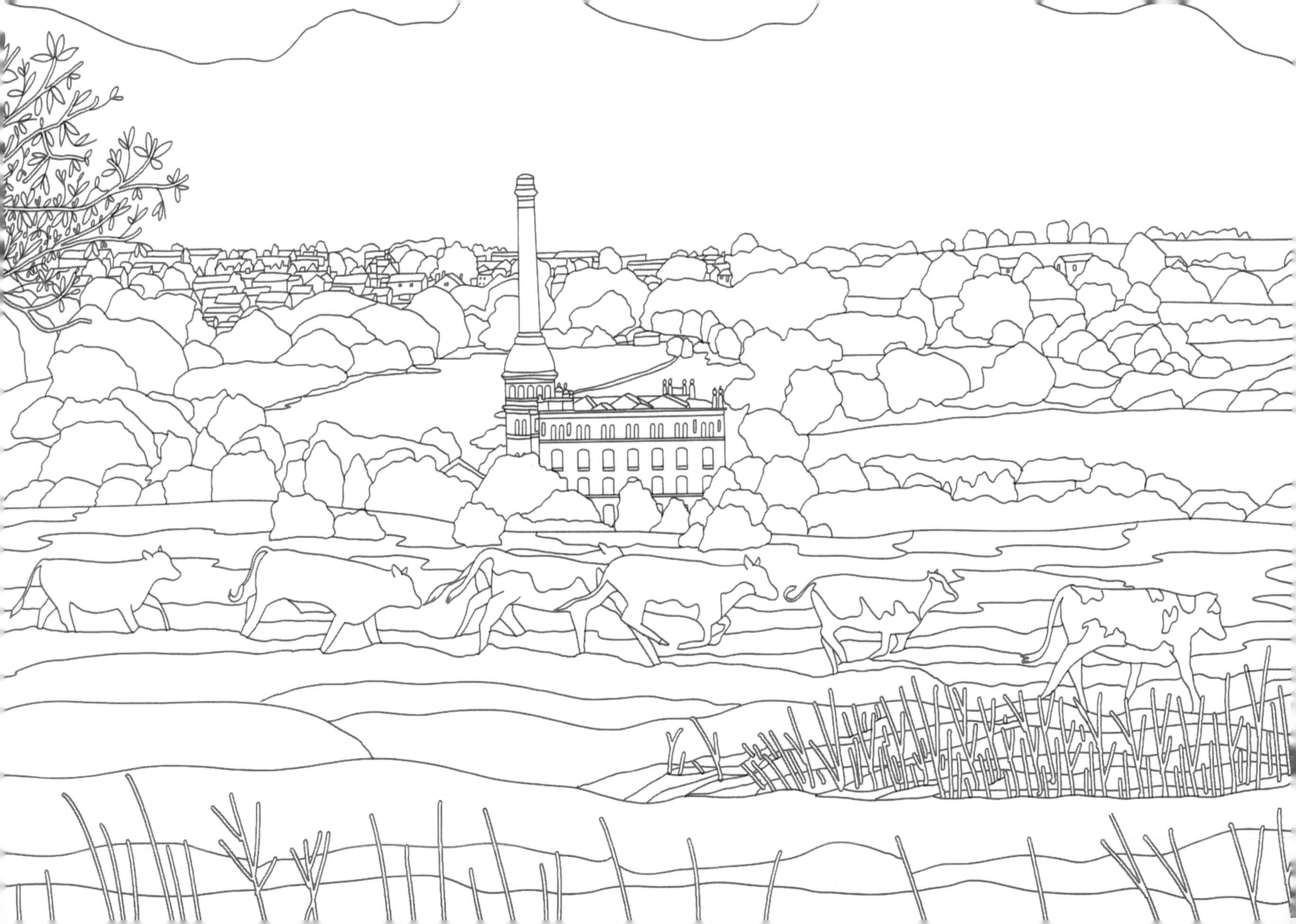

A peacock at Harcourt Arboretum, Oxford ▸

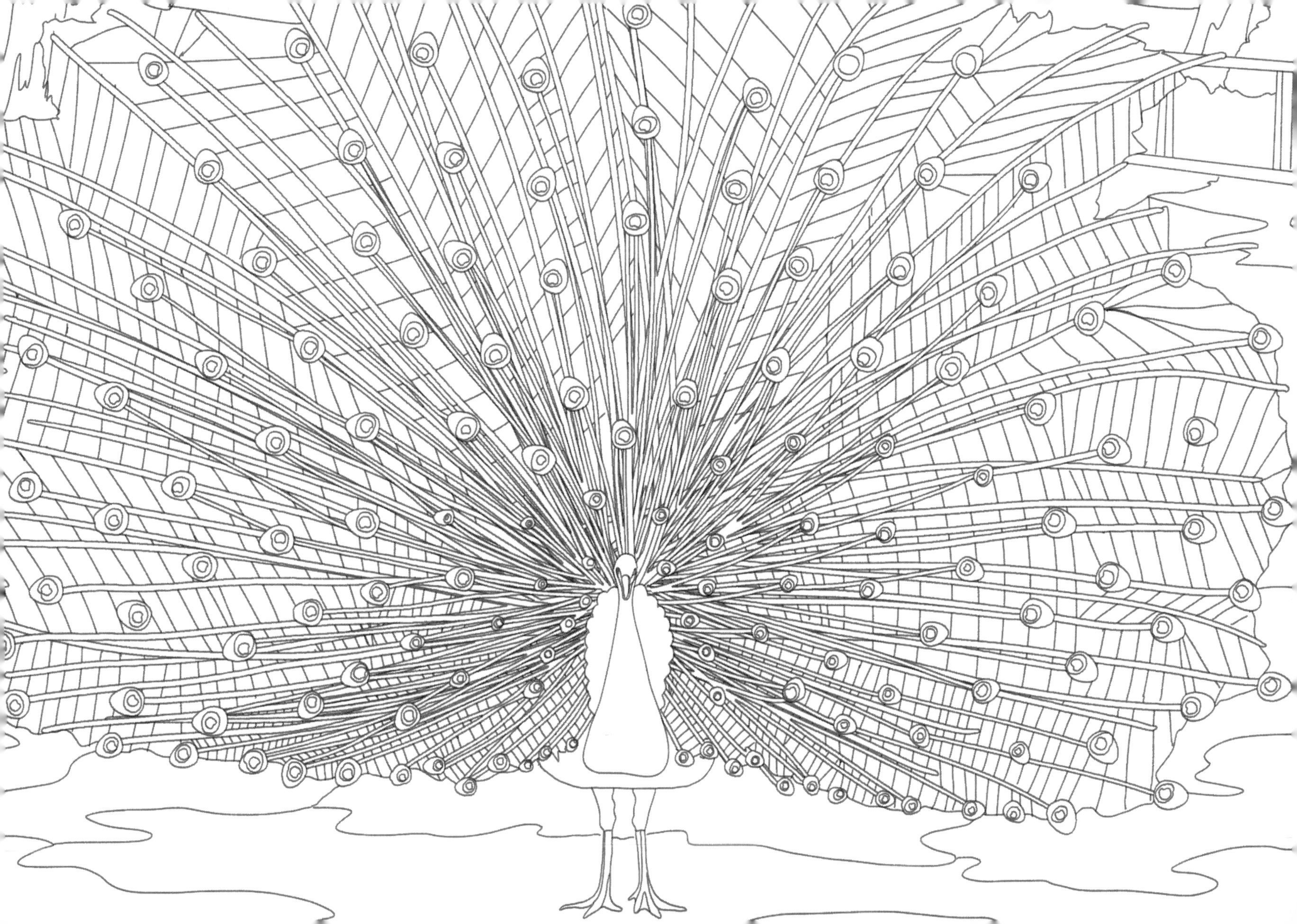

The Pitt Rivers Museum, Oxford ▸

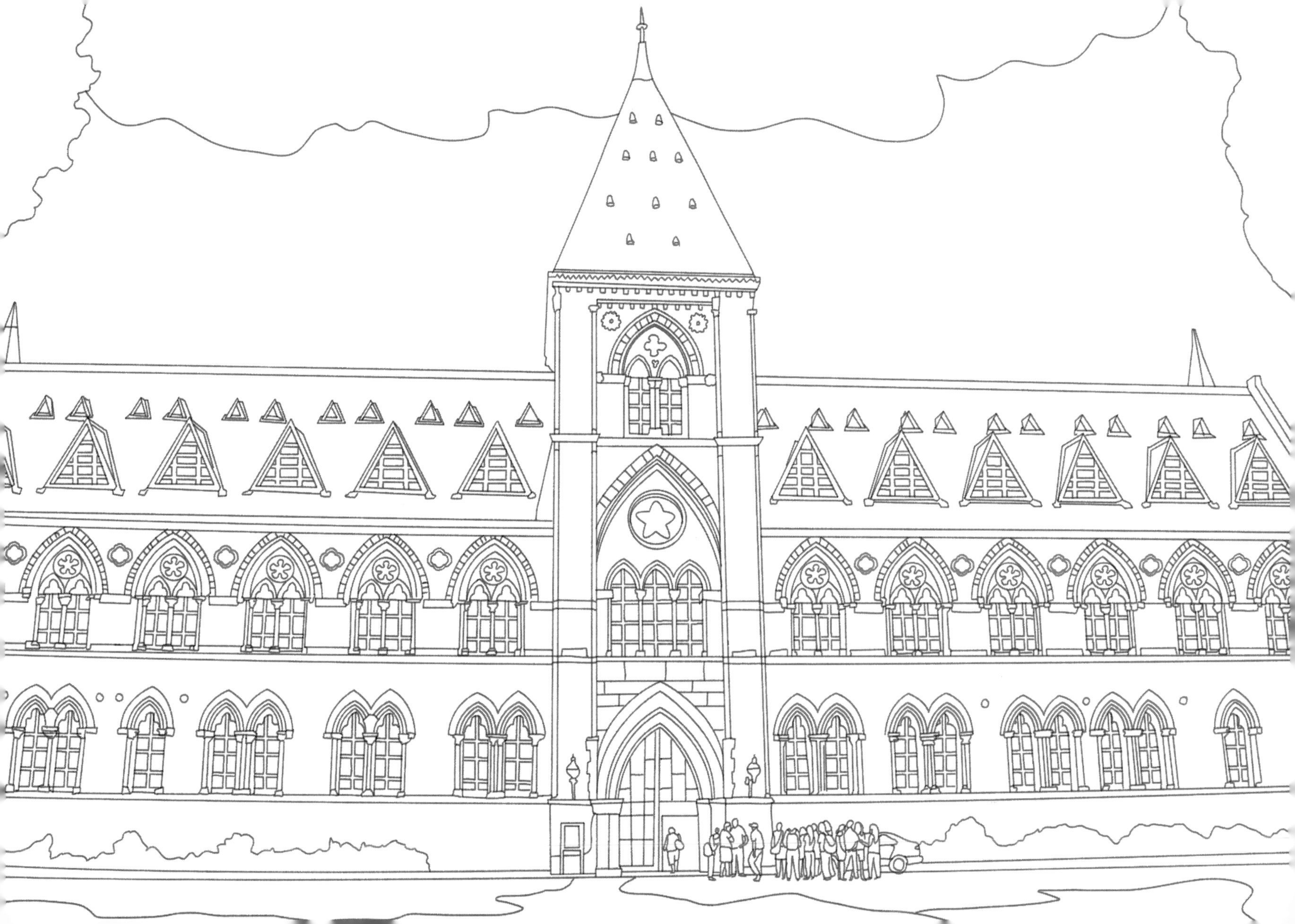

The Rollright Stones, near Chipping Norton ▸

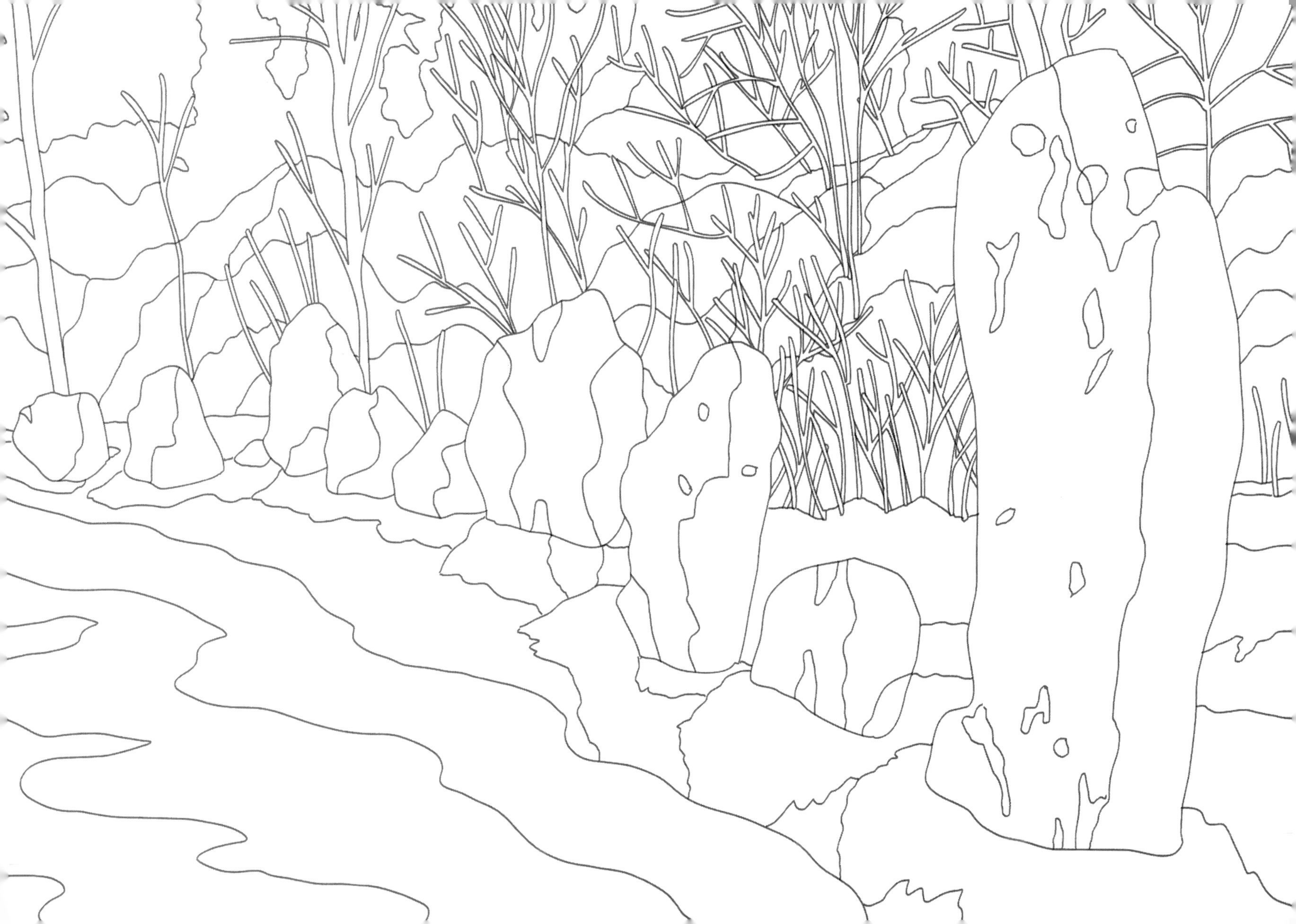

St Helen's Wharf, Abingdon, c. 1910 ▶

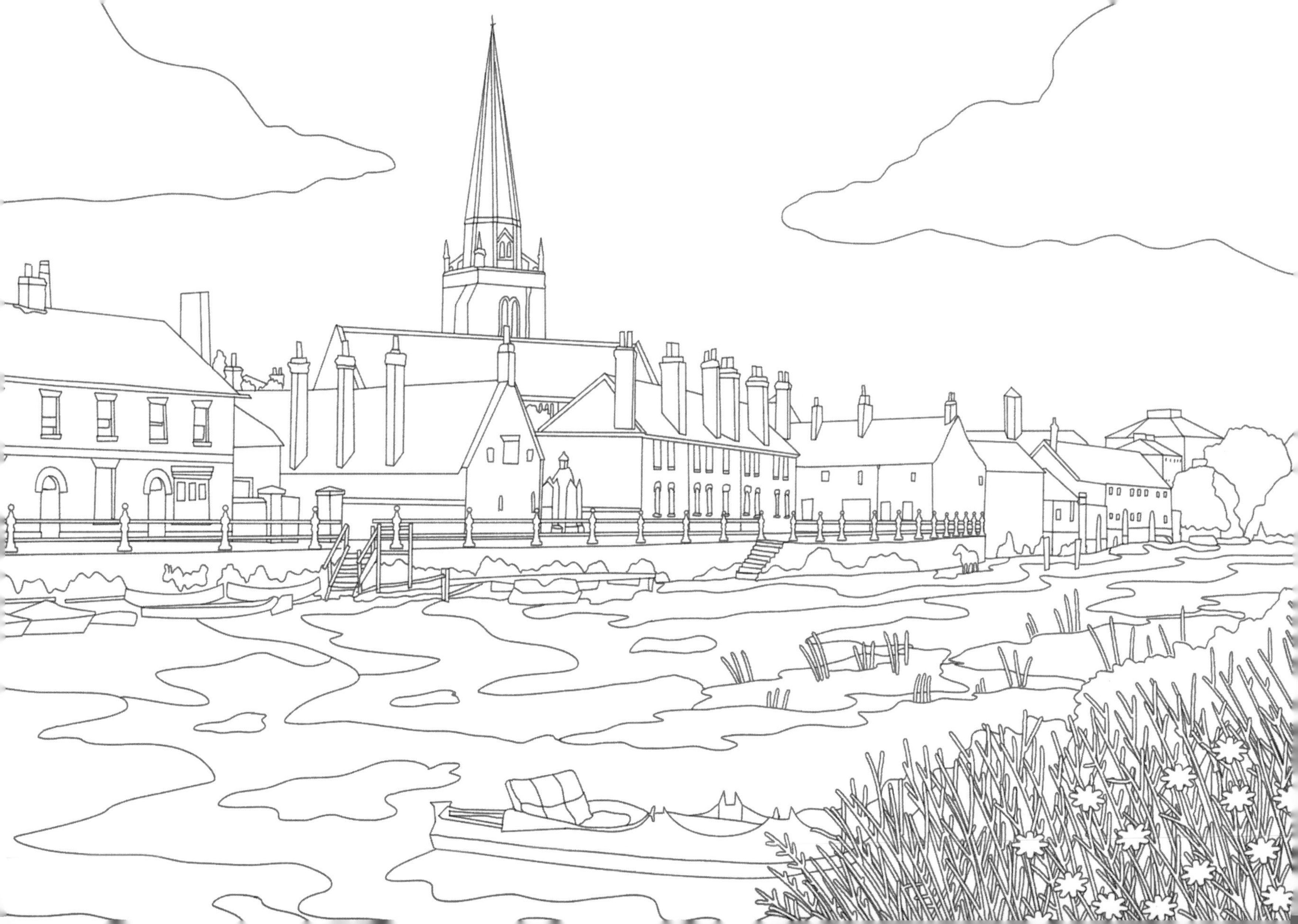

Didcot Railway Centre ▶

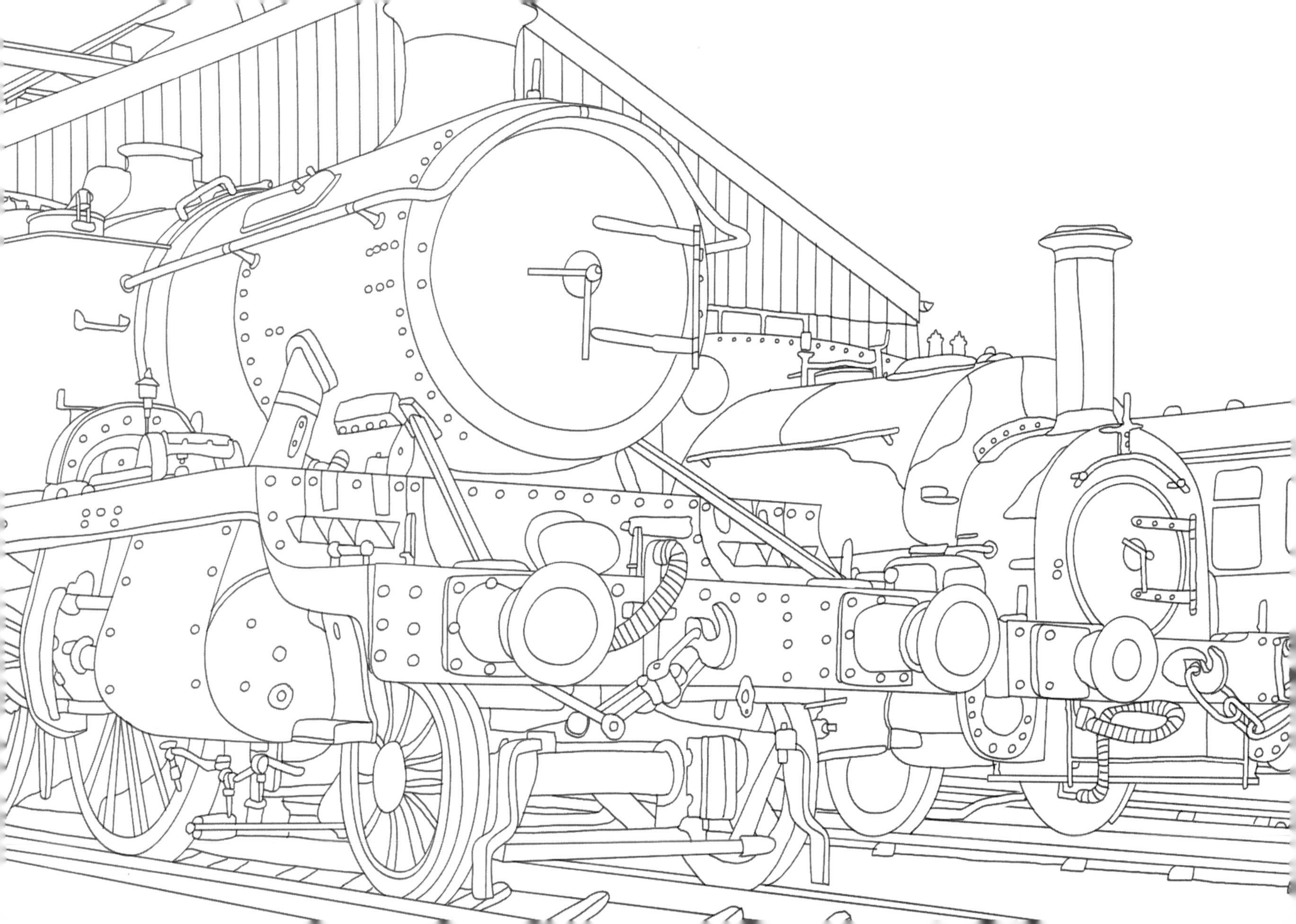

The Bridge of Sighs links the two halves of Hertford College across New College Lane, Oxford ▸

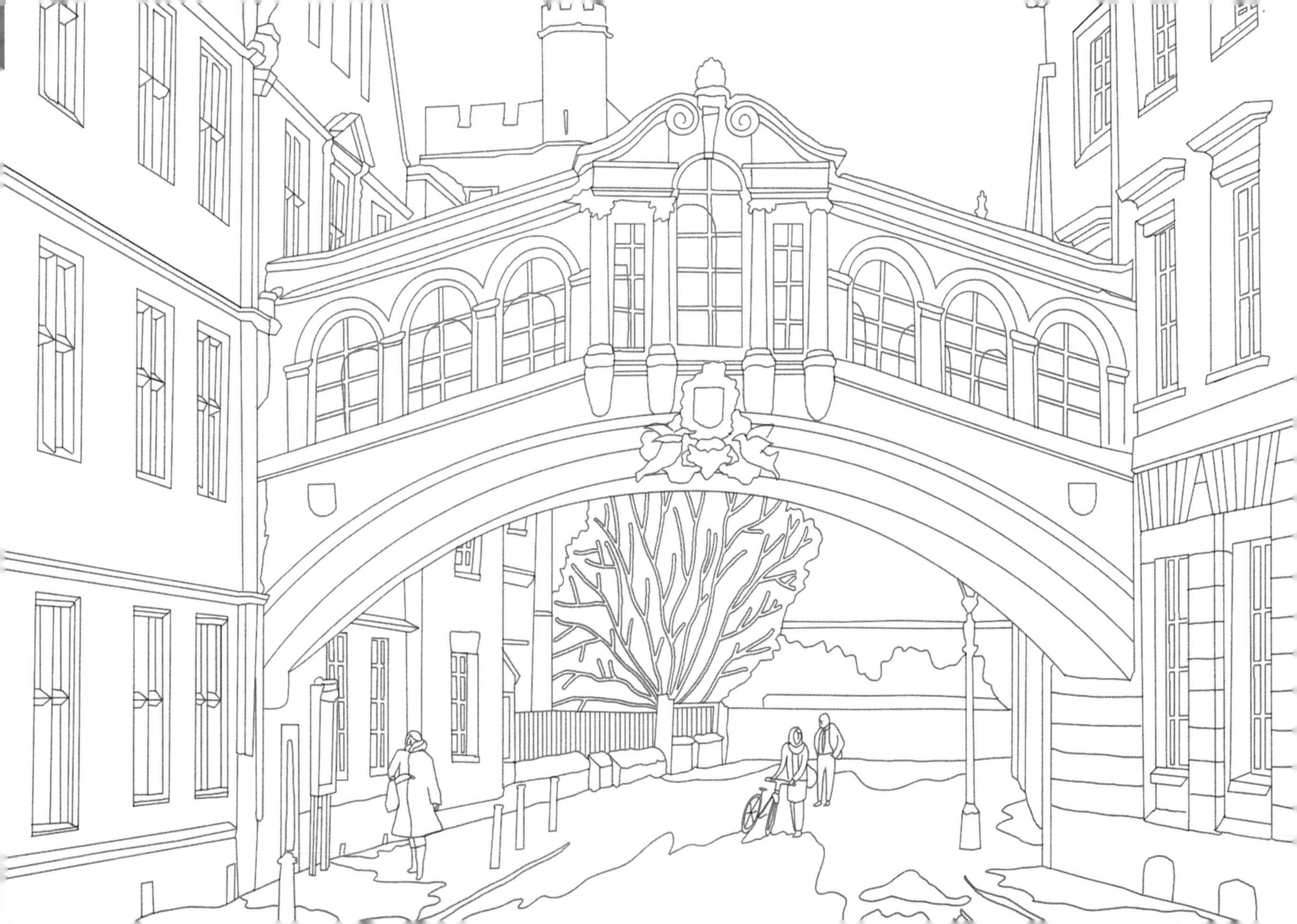

The Market Place and statue of
King Alfred, Wantage, *c.* 1909 ▶

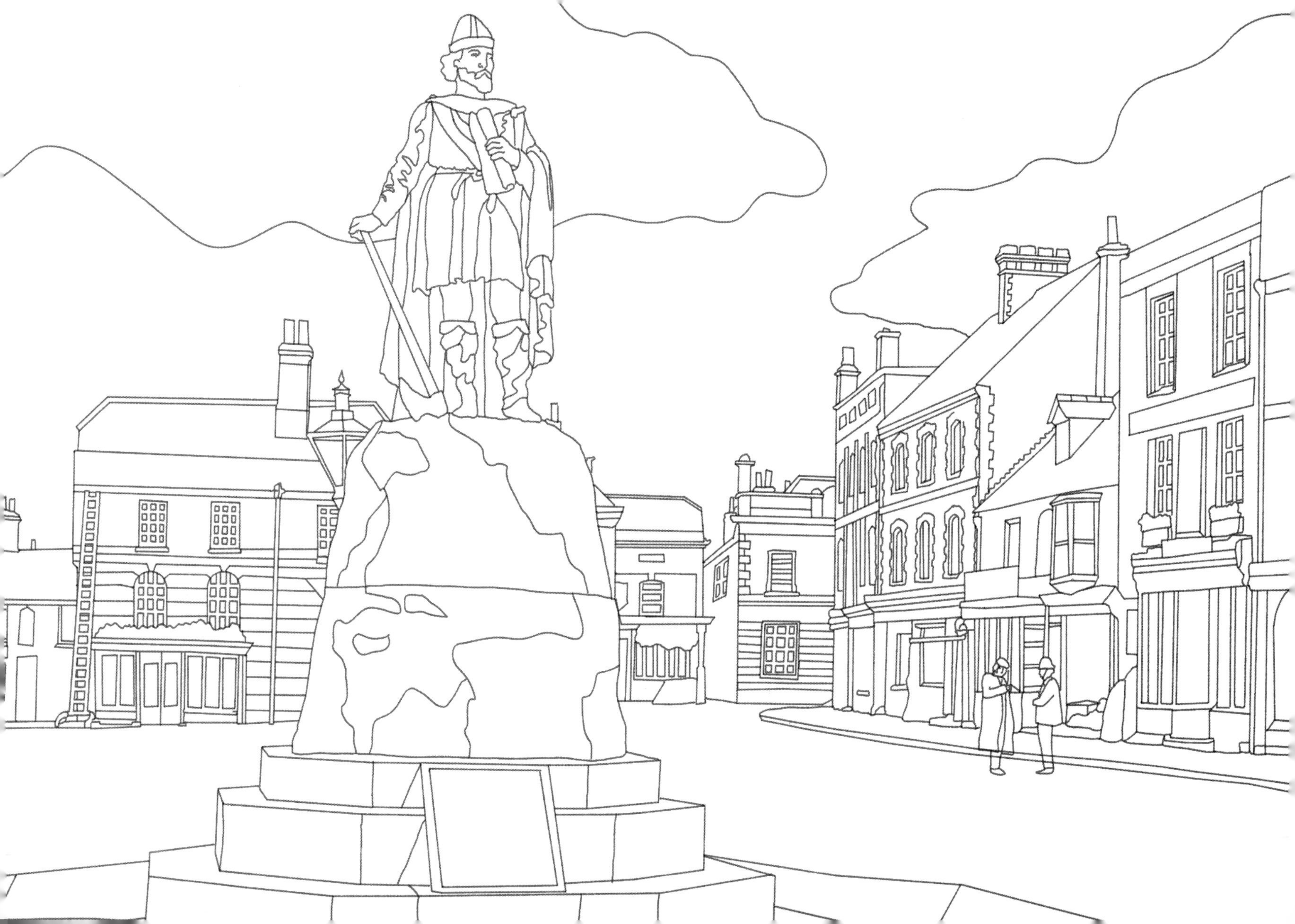

The Radcliffe Camera, now part
of the Bodleian Library, Oxford ▸

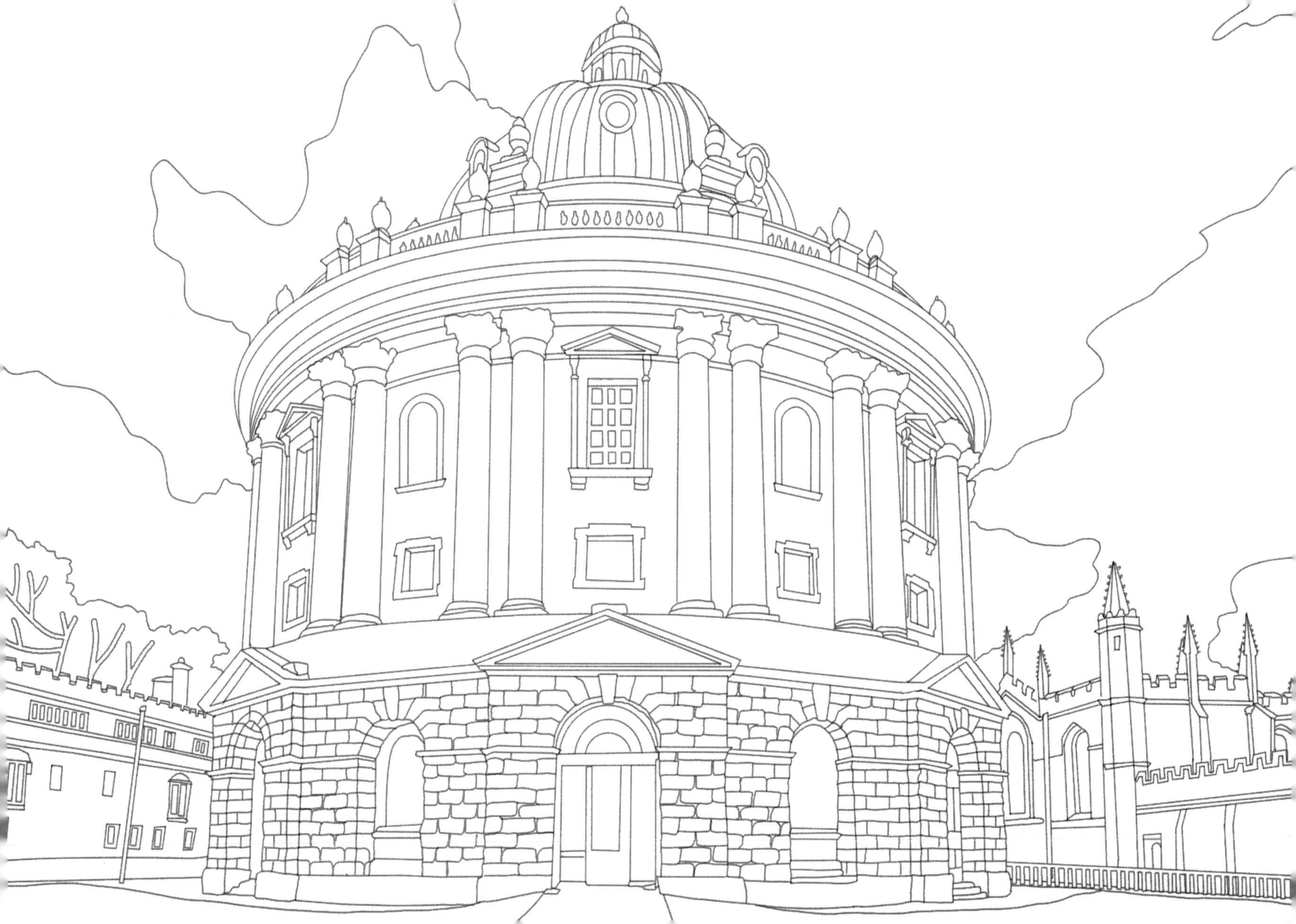

University College Men's 1ˢᵗ VIII ▸

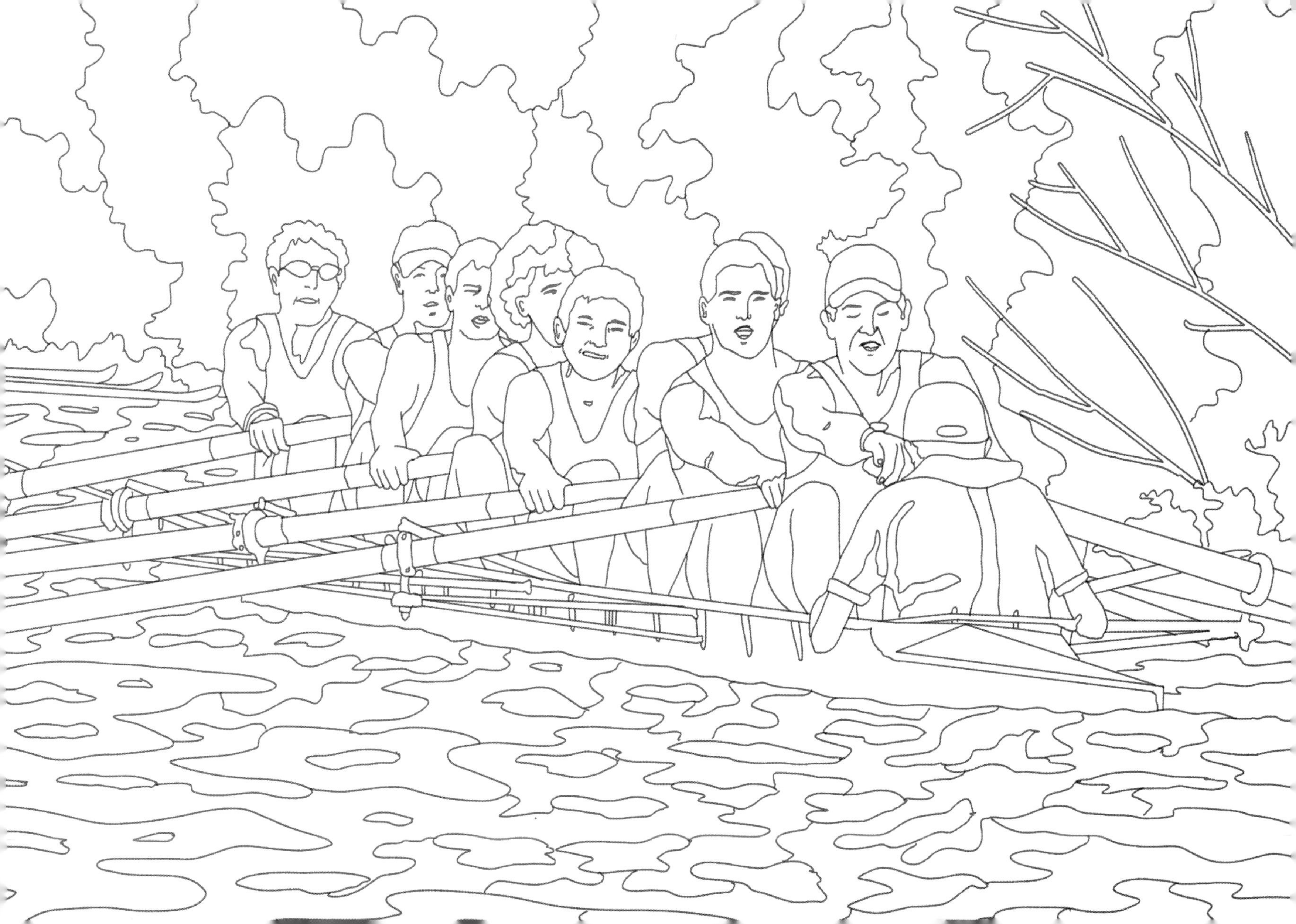

The River Thames and Abingdon church spire ▸

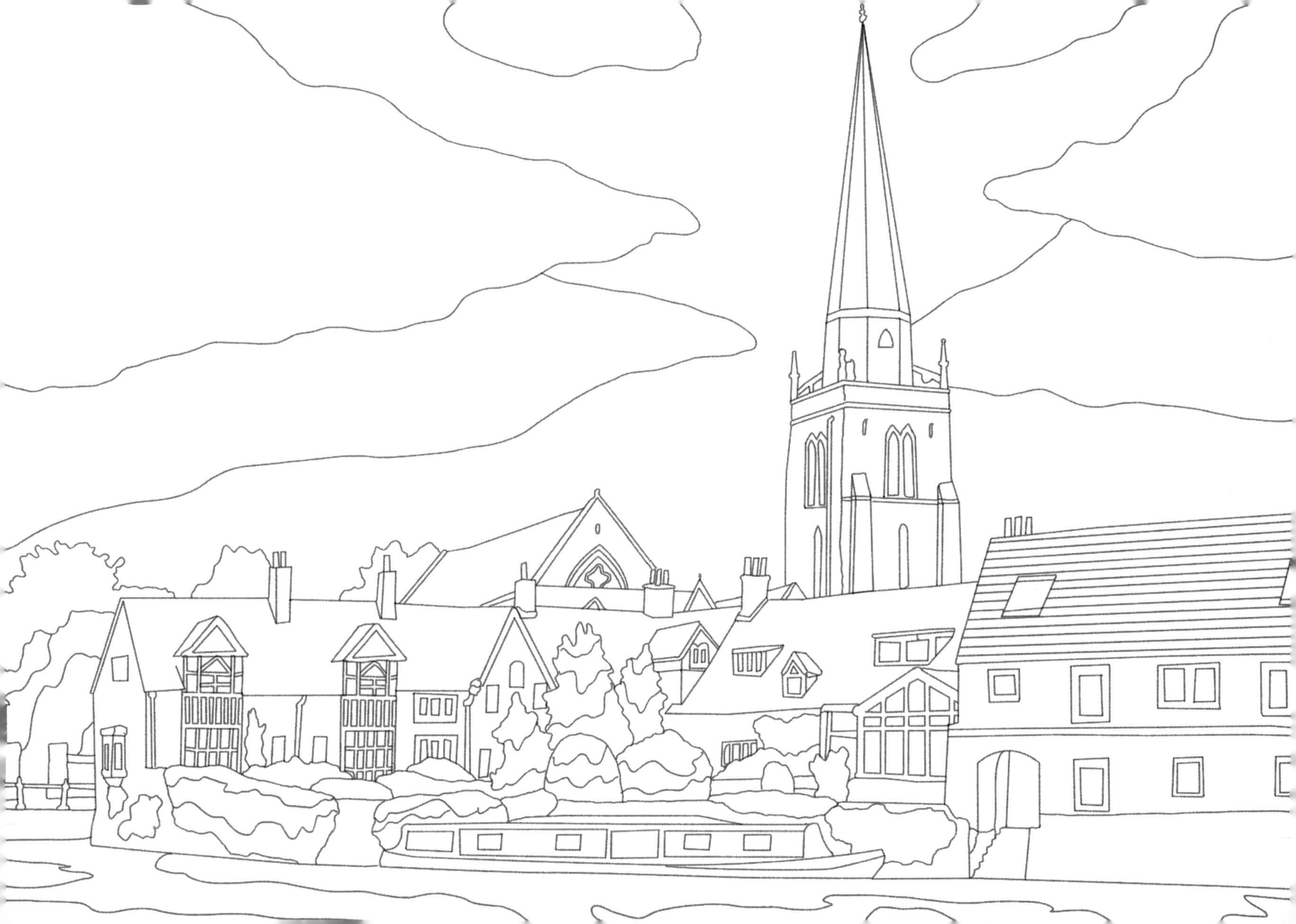

Tuesday market at Thame, 1963 ▸

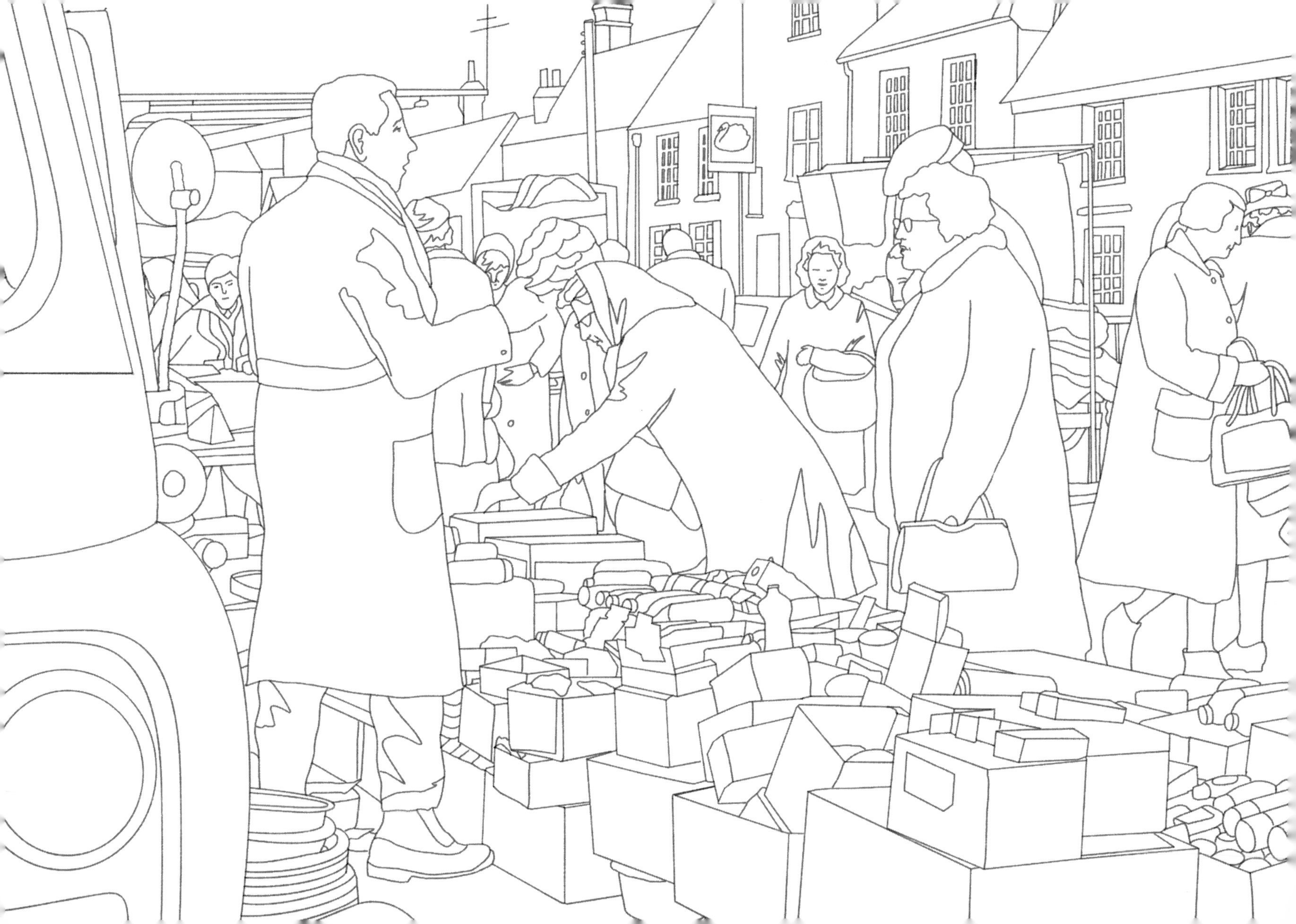

The Uffington White Horse ▶

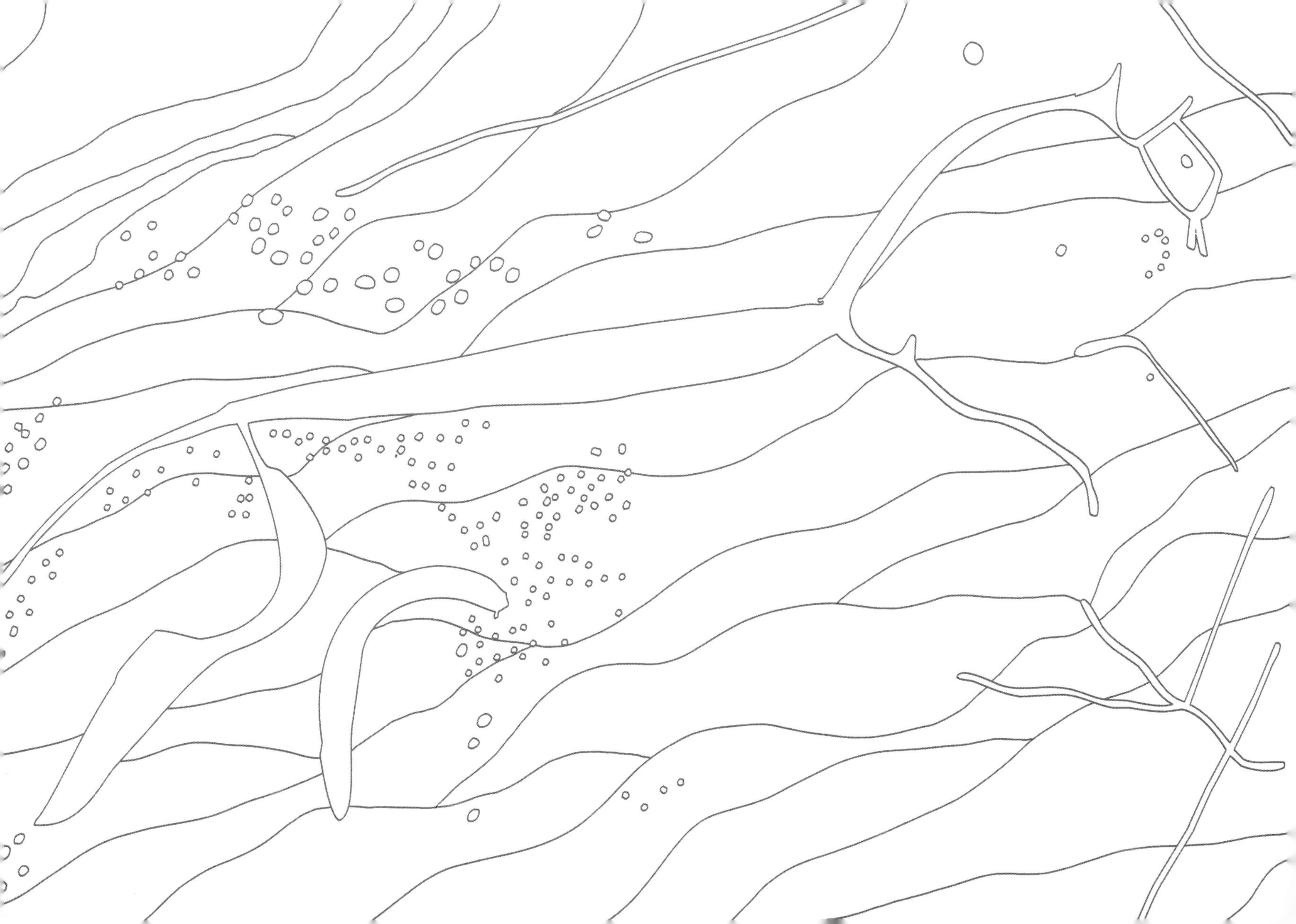

The Leander crew at Henley Regatta, 1890s ▶

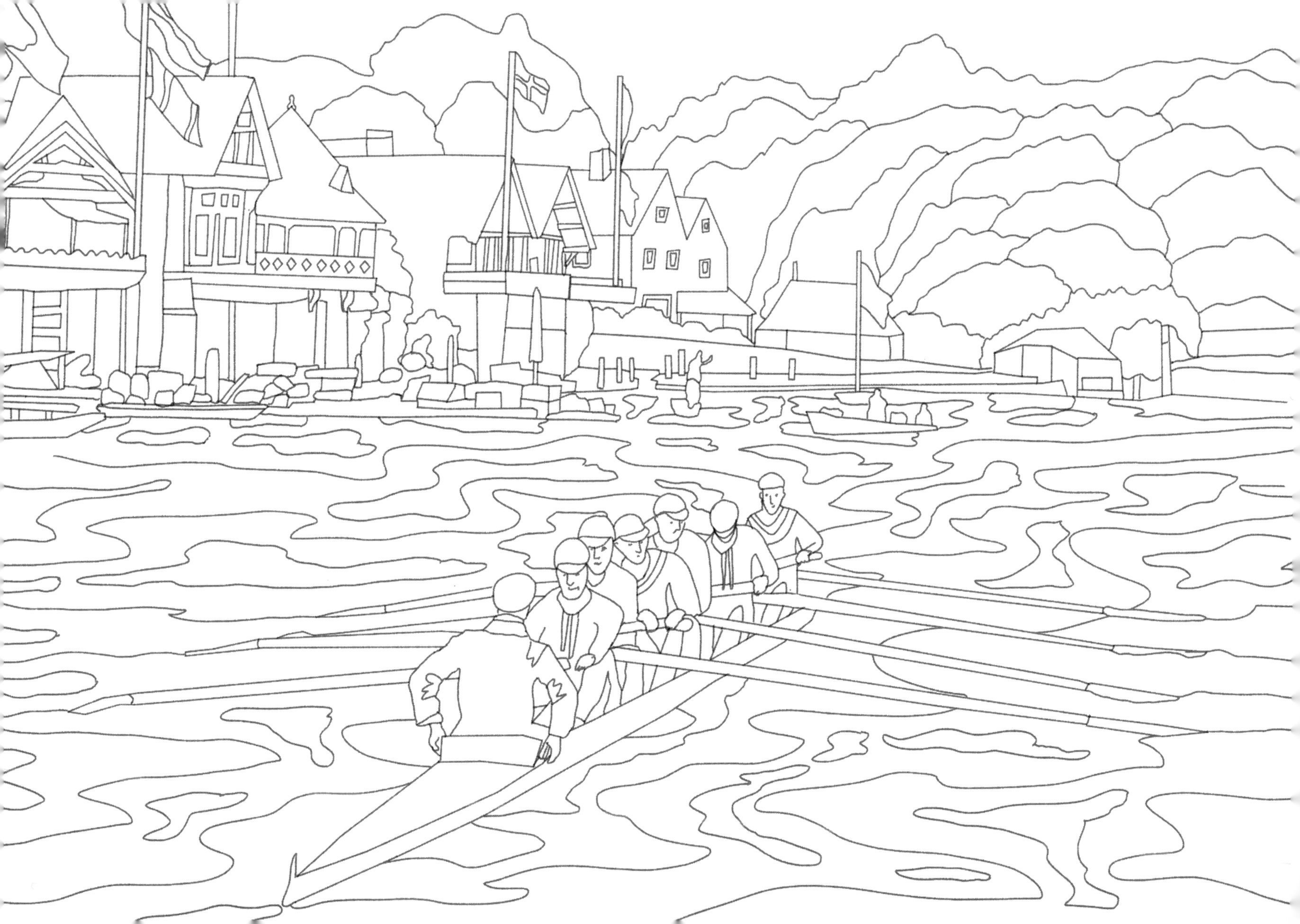

St Michael at the North Gate, Oxford ▶

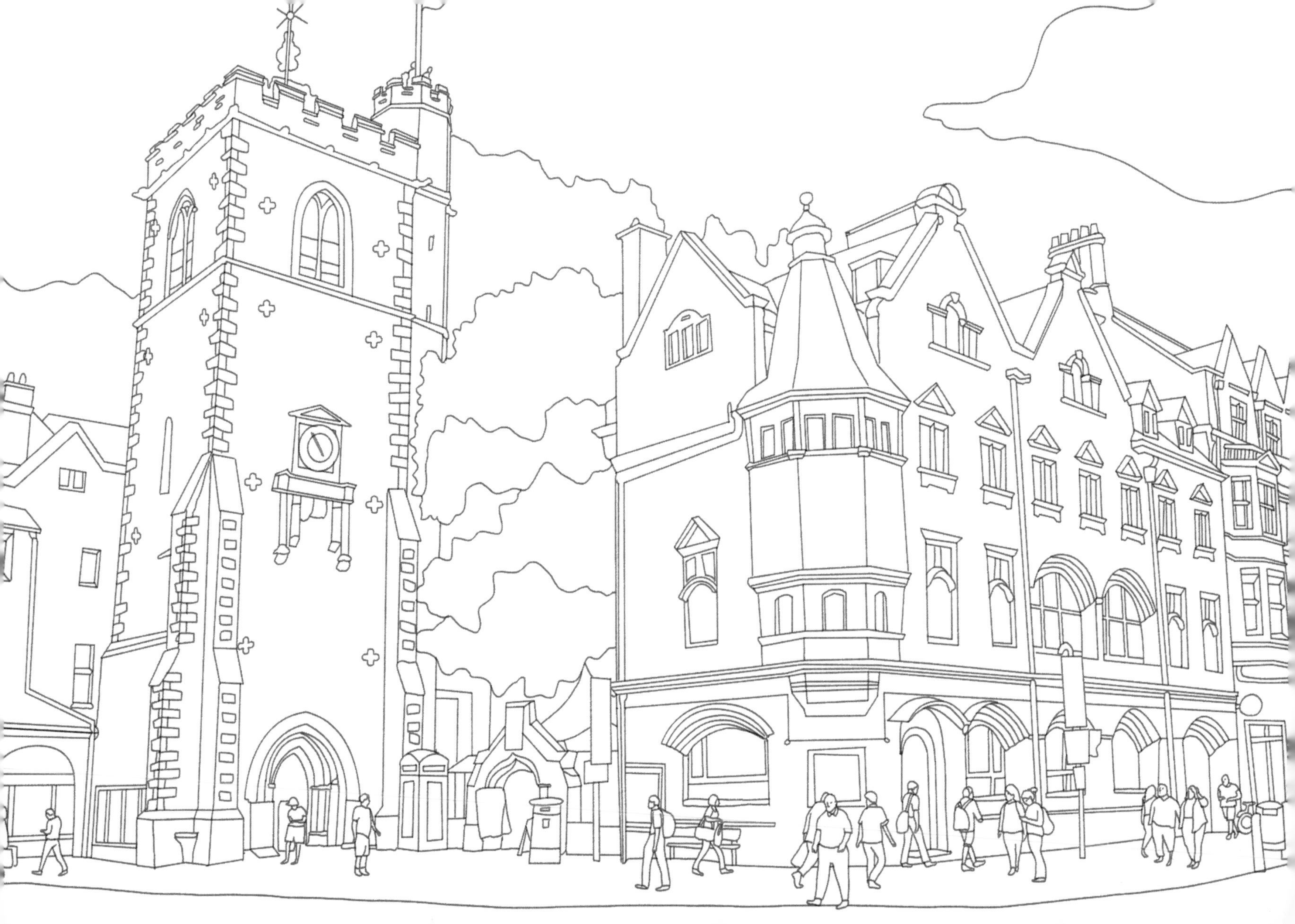

Sightseeing in Oxford ▶

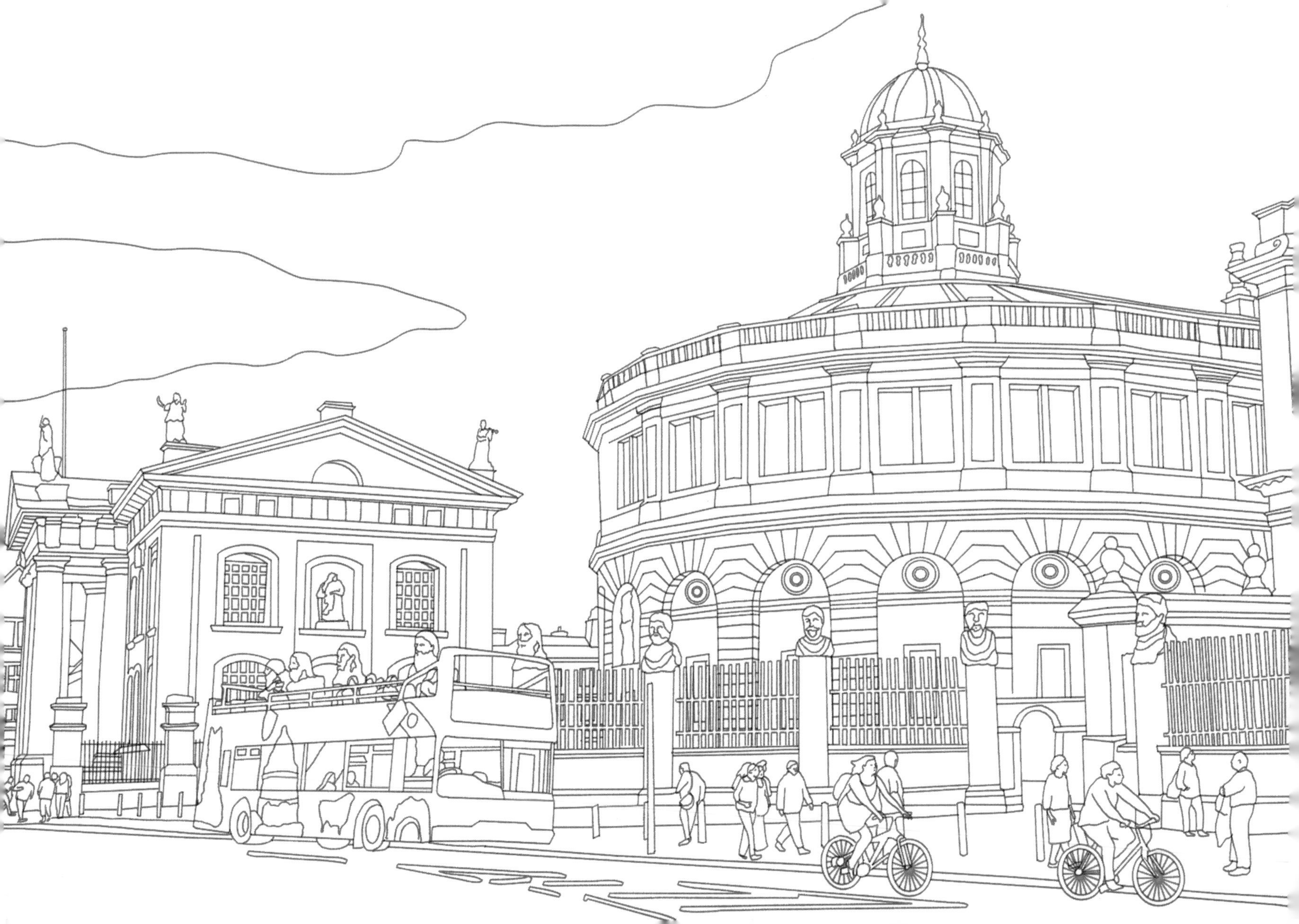

Morris dancers at Oxford Folk Weekend ▸

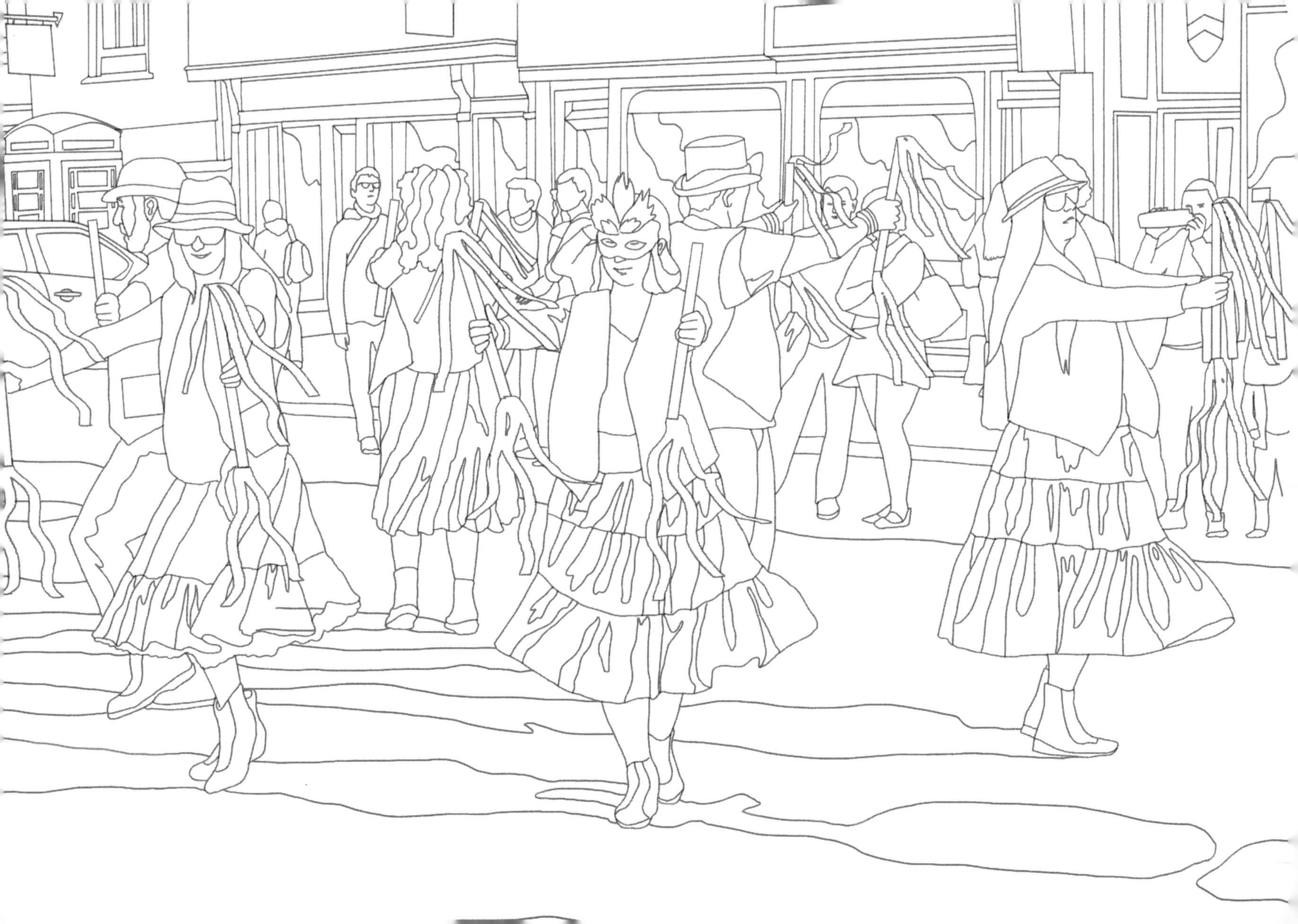

Vintage bus at the Oxford Bus
Museum, Long Hanborough ▶

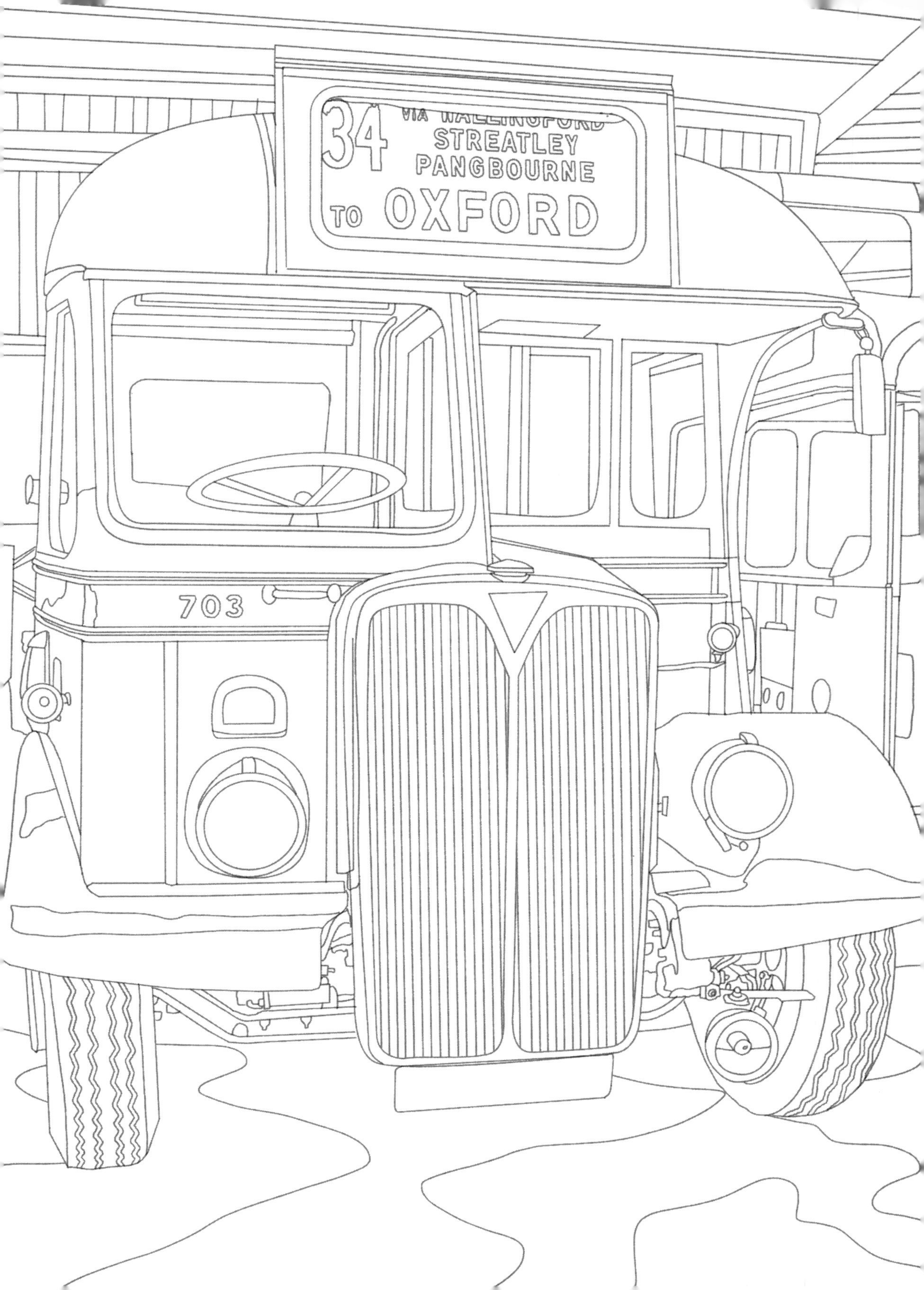
34
STREATLEY
PANGBOURNE
TO OXFORD
703

Ashbury village ▶

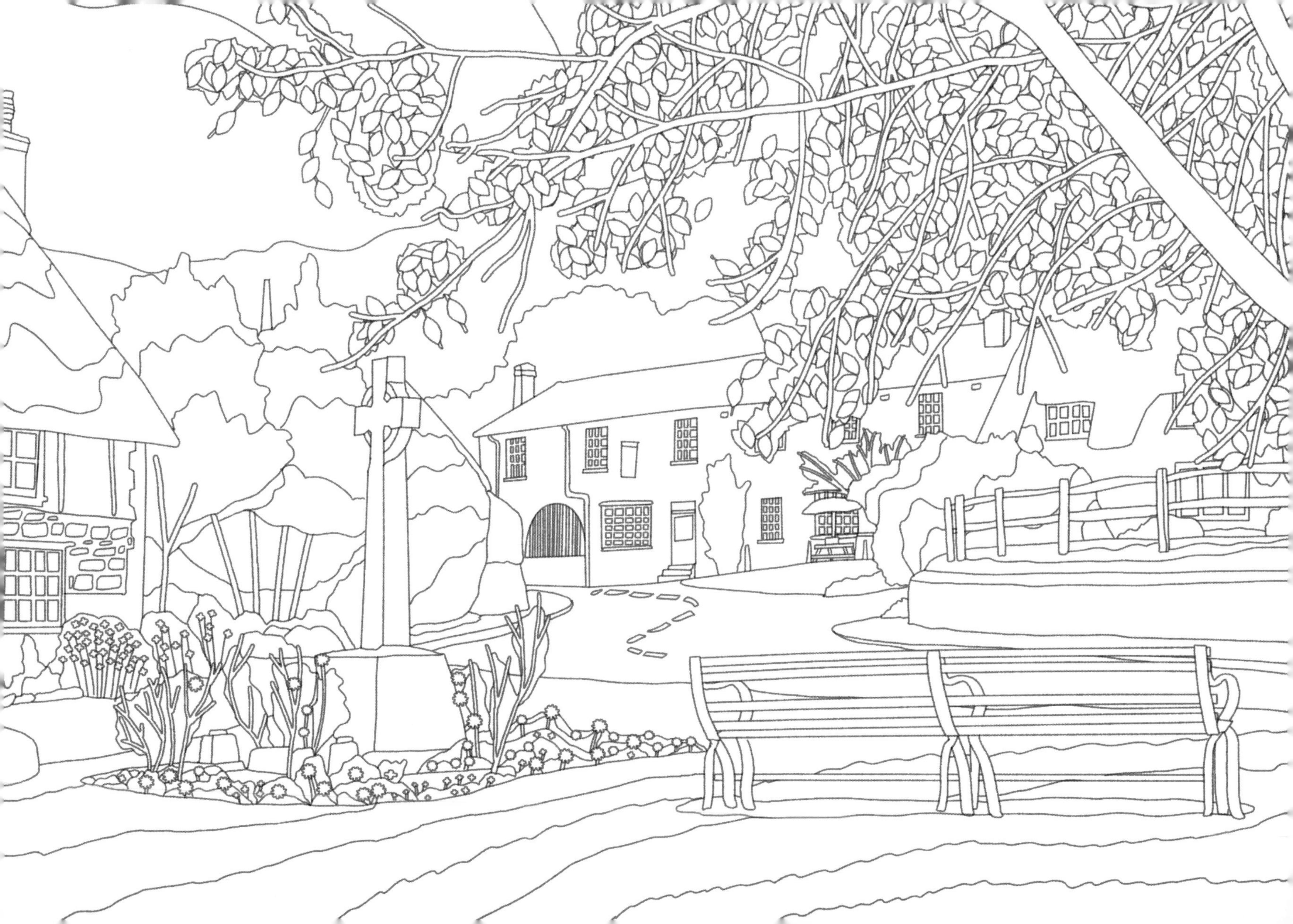

Waterperry House, Gardens and
Garden Centre, near Wheatley ▶

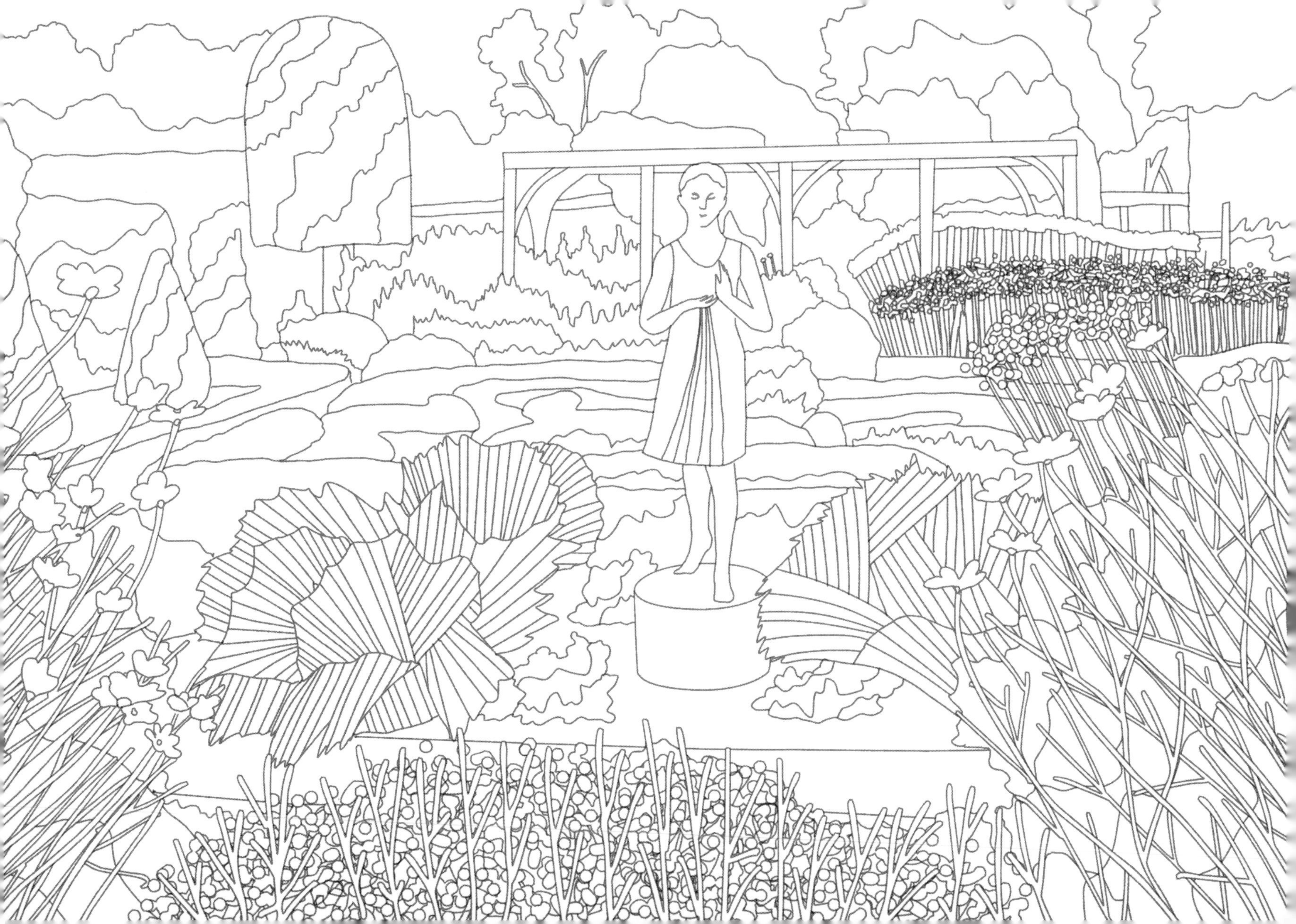

The Eagle and Child pub in Oxford is best known for
being the watering hole for C.S. Lewis and J.R.R. Tolkien ▸

The Eagle and Child

Also from The History Press

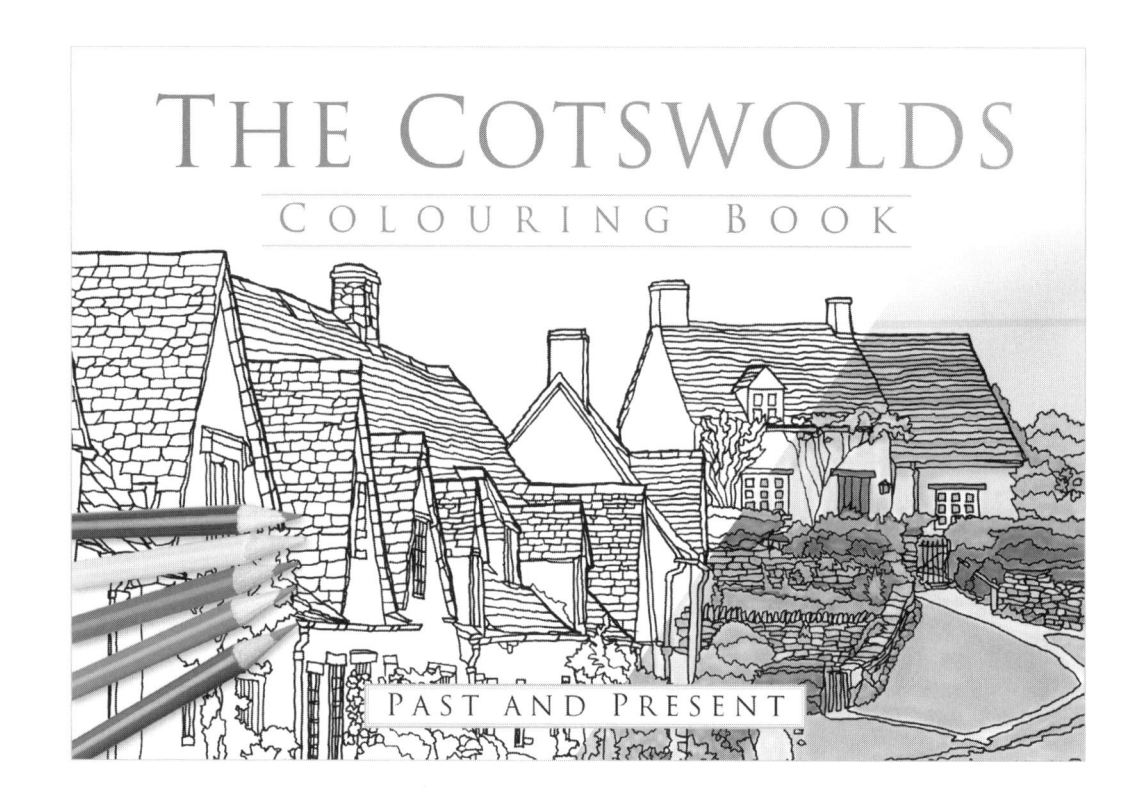

# THE COTSWOLDS
## COLOURING BOOK
### PAST AND PRESENT

Find this colouring book and more at
**www.thehistorypress.co.uk**